PEOPLE AND LEGENDS OF HIMALAYA AND THE GANGA

PEOPLE AND LEGENDS OF HIMALAYA AND THE GANGA

M. P. Kuksal

Publications

KALPAZ PUBLICATIONS

DELHI-110052

People and Legends of Himalaya and the Ganga

Rs. 690

ISBN : 81-7835-594-9

Published in 2007 in India by
Kalpaz Publications
C-30, Satyawati Nagar, Delhi-110052
Phone : 9212729499
E-mail : Kalpaz@hotmail. com

Laser Typesetting at : Master Computers, Delhi
Printed at : Salasar Imaging System, Delhi

This book is dedicated to my son,
Ashok
who left us in the prime of his youth.

The Parting Smile

In Memory of my Son, Ashok

In prime of youth, in spring of life,
You left us in a tragic plight,
In bloom of life so young and bright.

Your face still had your natural smile,
From where it came to just beguile,
When life within had ceased to shine.

A jewel of life, you were unmatched,
A blooming flower untimely snatched,
The strings of life suddenly snapped.

With melancholy heart I went in search.
Bewildered in this gloomy earth,
Like search of a needle in vast desert.

I searched you in the words of sages,
I searched you in celestial pages,
I searched you in scriptures of ages.

No one could tell where you had gone,
Leaving me here a life to mourn,
Oh! God for all this was I born.

Years of search, a search futile,
Weary, exhausted, unreconciled,
I laid my arms and paused a while.

Then suddenly one day I glimpsed you clear,
In sweet face of my grand daughter dear,
When she was playing with me quite near.

I saw you peeping through her eyes,
A face true replica of thine,
As you were once true self of mine.

You were then seen in wider light,
In children young, innocent, bright,
Your smile divine in all alike.

I see your smile in roses bright,
That blossom with the spring's delight,
Scattering perfume all day and night.

I see your smile in fresh dawn's light,
That melts the stars of dark blue night,
And drives sun's chariot in sky so bright.

Deep in my bosom I feel your smile,
Imperceptible creeping with all its light,
A glow to brush my gloom aside.

Your smile forever with me I know,
It follows me wherever I go,
And makes life easy, smooth and slow.

In long summer days in long wintry nights,
When quite alone none by my side,
It leaves me never in lonely plight.

Now every smile to me is bliss,
A heavenly shower a godly kiss,
A path divine I never miss.

Oh! God this boon I only pray,
That I may cross my ending mile,
With your image and just a smile.

Contents

Foreword

Compellingly powerful, the account opens a window to the glory of our mighty Himalayas with a lucid glimpse of myth, history and belief as well as unending series of kaleidoscopic colourful changes occurring throughout the narrative. It is a journeying into the dazzling radiency of the Swarg Lok where Lord Indra in company with lesser gods drinks Amrit the nectar of life.

It also deals in a down-to-earth description of great constructive changes that have been brought about by the untiring efforts of the author and of men like him who have been responsible for improving the social fabric of life within the region.

Written in a simple Gandhian style, the author deals with folklore, culture, agriculture and horticulture in the land. A land where as simple and charming a people as one can find anywhere has lived ever since the dawn of civilization.

However, there remains a latent vein of sadness at times brought to light by the author's inconsolable loss of those who have been dear to him.

The entire study is a sincere contribution and is well calculated to draw the reader closer to our heritage. Equipped with it the tourists triumph could be complete.

Sirdar Mohamed Osman
(Wild-Lifer, Naturalist, Geophysicist
and freelance Journalist)

Author of
Hunters of the Air (publisher W. W. F. India)
Falcony in the Land of the Sun. (publisher Western Sporting Ranch ester W.Y. U. S. A.)
Musings of an Afgan Falconer (publisher Kenyon Gibson London)
The Bonellis Eagle. (publisher Gibson London).

Acknowledgements

This book is the outcome of inspiration given to me by my daughters, sons-in-law, daughter-in-law, grandsons and their wives, grand daughters Meetu, Priyanka and her husband Tarun. They pressed me to write the reminiscences of my life which I often related to them during long winter nights.

I am grateful to Mr R. C. Pandey, Sirdar Mohamed Osman and Mr Raghuraj Singh for their valuable suggestions and going through the manuscript. I appreciate the help I got from Sidharth and Pallavi and encouragement I got from Lieutenant Colonel B. S. Rawat from time to time.

M. P. Kuksal
31 Teg Bahadur Road, Lane 3
Dehradun.

Introduction

My heart leaps up when I behold,
A rainbow in the sky.
So was it when my life began,
So is it now I am a man,
So be it when I shall grow old.
(W. Wordsworth)

Like the heart of the poet which thrills at the sight of the rainbow in the sky my heart throbs with joy when I see the majestic snow peaks of the Himalayas.

The picturesque Garhwal and Kumaon hills with their small villages, simple village folk, alpine meadows, flowers, dazzling snow peaks have been my whole world. Through the medium of these lines I wish to renew the forgotten hours of my life. I look back with pleasure to the time I spent roaming the Himalayas. It is with a sense of deep gratitude to our Maker who in his benevolence bestowed on me the privilege to accomplish all this.

With the passage of time memory tends to fade away. It primarily is to avoid such gaps in remembrance that events and incidents have for the benefit of the reader been arrested from fading. It is an attempt to preserve

Garhwal's pristine beauty, the purity, the rustic charm of its kind and hospitable people, all these and much more, for the coming generations to know. If it happens to meet these requirements I will feel amply rewarded.

M. P. Kuksal

1

The Divine Himalayas

The Himalayas lure me, inspire me, and attract me to their bosom saying, "This is your eternal abode". The sight of snow peaks has excited me since childhood. A sweet, homely feeling creeps into my heart and I feel like running to them, to home, sweet home. I still recall vividly when as a student in junior classes in Nainital, I often climbed up the Snow View hill to reach its top and marvel at the white snow range in the far distance. Sitting under some tree, I would muse for hours and wish I was a bird that could fly over distant hills and reach the perennial snow. Would a day ever come into my life when I could see them close by, walk by their side, climb them and fill my heart with their grandeur, majesty and immensity? What was then a child's dream became reality in later life. God granted my earnest wish and I wandered over the mighty Himalayas for over sixteen years of my life. I had the fortune to visit Gangotri, Gaumukh, Tapovan, Neelang, Pulumsunda, Deodital, Dayara and Gidara bugyals in Uttarkashi district and Kedarnath, Tungnath, Rudranath, Badrinath, Valley of Flowers, Hemkund Lokpal, The Niti Valley and Hotidhura in Chamoli district. It was a clear morning of June 1956, when I was atop the Hotidhura (18,500 feet) with some companions. What a panoramic view greeted my eyes! The lofty Himalayan peaks to the South and the great Tunjunla and the Tibetan plateau in the North. The white snow peaks were glittering in the morning sun and I was lost in their super grandeur. What a great contrast nature presented before me! I saw the massive rugged mountains with their bright snow peaks on the South, the Indian side, and the green velvety plateau of Tibet, in the North. Traders told me that when their horses reach the top they virtually run towards the green pastures of Tibet and it is difficult to control them.

I have captured the majestic beauty of Himalayan snow peaks from different angles and places. I have often seen them from the outermost high hills and I have watched them closely from their base. I have bathed in their beauty in summer, autumn, winter and spring. They have given me divine sensation, aroused celestial emotions and have filled my heart with a bliss that is beyond expression. A wide snow range is seen from the hilltops of Chakrata, Mussoorie, Pauri Lansdowne, Ranikhet and Almora towns of Uttaranchal. The best view is seen from Pauri. On a clear day, especially after rains, when the sky is free of mist and dust, one can easily locate all the peaks-right from Bandarpooch in the far West to Nanda Devi in the East. You see Bandarpooch, Srikanth, Shivling, Chaukhamba, Hathi and Ghori Parvat, The Kamet, The Dronagiri, Trisul and the beautiful Nanda Devi peak. I have seen the legendary Dronagiri closely from its base. It looks like the throne of a mighty king. A huge chunk seems to be missing from its central part and the exposed surface appears crimson. The villagers told me that it was this part which had Sanjiveny herb(a life saving plant). Hanuman, who was in a great hurry, found difficult to discover it, carved out the entire portion, which was full of medicinal herbs including the Sanjivani and flew away with it to Lanka, to save the life of Laxman who was lying unconscious on the battlefield. The red colour, they told me was the blood of the mountain. This is the unchanging faith of the simple village folk down the ages. The serenity of the Neelkanth peak, the-Queen of the Himalayan Mountains, is best observed from the Nar Parvat side of Badrinath. Neelkanth is named after the blue tinged throat of lord Shiva who drank the deadly poison, Kalkoot, churned out of the ocean. Shiva retained the poison in his throat and saved the gods and demons collected there to churn the ocean. The blue dome of the peak glitters in the sun and gives it a mystic aura. The celestial beauty of the group of peaks, namely the Bhagirath 1, Bhagirath 2, Bhagirath 3, the Shivling peak, the Chaturangi peak is best seen from their base near Tapovan, a unique flat area on the left flank of Gaumukh glacier. The Gaumukh glacier gives an appearance of the matted hair of Lord Shiva from where, the Puranas say, Mother Ganga could not find her way out. Bhagirath prayed to Shiva who allowed her to come out. The glacier stretches for miles but due to global warming and pollution, is receding at an alarming pace. Urgent efforts are needed to check this environmental calamity.

The closest and the best view of the Central Himalaya is seen from Gorson bugyal about 10 km from Joshimath. For the more adventurous, a difficult trek to the Kuanri Pass is well worth the effort as the view is wider and unmatched in its splendour. Gorson is the now famous Auli-Gorson skiing spot in Chamoli district. Kuanri pass is on the old trekking route from Gwaldom to Joshimath. From Gwaldom the route passes through Wan, Dewal, Kanol, Sutol, Ramni, Gauna, Pana and is then a very tough climb to Kuanri pass, which is 10,000 feet above sea level. The route passes through different elevations. From the high hills of Gwaldom there is a big drop to the Pindar valley then again a steep climb to Kanol, which is covered with thick deodar and Kail forests. There is again a descent to the Nandakini River near village Sutol which is on the right bank of the Nandakini. From Sutol it is a gradual climb to village Ghoni and Ramni. Ramni is a big village at a height of 6,000 feet above sea level and is famous for its good quality of barley, which was once called Ramni variety by the Agriculture Department. The area also has good quality of slate, rock used for covering the roofs. There is a Zila Parishad dak bungalow where I have often enjoyed a day's rest during my frequent tours. To the East you see a magnificent view of distant green hills and the alpine meadows of Bedini Bugyal, which is on the way to Roopkund. The Ramni top gives a close view of the Himalayas. Villagers told me that in the olden days several foreign trekkers came that way. The area was humming with activity during summer and autumn. Now nobody comes. It may be due to the restrictions on foreigners in this sensitive area, bordering Tibet.

From Ramni you have to walk down to Gauna where a massive lake had formed in the year 1893 due to a huge blockage in Birahi River. The lake which at one time was a tourist's paradise, having more than it's share of the trout fish, met an untimely demise when it spilled over because of heavy rains and silting in the year 1970. A steep climb from Gauna and village Pana takes one to the Kuanri Pass. Kuanri pass gives the most commanding, closest and best view of the central Himalayas. On a clear blue day especially after the rains in autumn one can see a galaxy of snow peaks straggling from Chaukhamba to Nandadevi. All peaks appear at arms length. You feel like touching them. The wrinkles formed on the snow are clearly visible to the naked eye. In front and to the left stand the four majestic pillars of Chaukhamba, next come the Neelkanth-Queen of the Himalaya and then the lofty Hathi and Ghori Parvat, to be followed by Kak Bhusandi, the Kamath and the Dronagiri peak.

There is a story in Ram Charitra Manas about a devout Brahmin who went to the ashram of sage Lomas at Sumeru Parvat. He requested the muni to teach him about devotion to Shagun Brahaman (The God with attributes). The sage taught him instead, devotion to Nirgun Brahman (God without attributes). The Brahmin's insistence on Shagun Brahman enraged the sage and he cursed him to become a crow. The Brahmin accepted the curse and lived like a crow with the sage in the Himalayas. The peak Kak Bhusandi is thus named after Kak Bhusandi, who subsequently related the story of Lord Ram to Garur.

The view of the lofty Himalaya is breathtaking. You see all the peaks at a glance from one end to the other and may repeat the exercise several times. Oh! What a feast to the eyes, mind, heart-nay to your whole self.

You find yourself lost in the Himalayan wonder. A heavenly bliss descends down to your heart and an imperceptible voice echoes within, "here is God in all its glory, in all its splendour and beauty." The words of Lord Krishna come to my mind "Among the mountains I am the Himalaya" (Geeta ch X). My eyes are now fixed on the blue dome of Neelkanth; calm and serene. I turn my eyes to the right towards a huge pile of snow, the great Alkapuri glacier beyond the Narayan Parvat, the treasure and the seat of Lord Kuber. I am reminded of the story of Yaksha in Kalidas's great poem, "Meghdoot". It was from here that Yaksha was banished and separated from his loving wife for a year, for dereliction of his duty by Kuber, his master.

Kalidas in his great epic "Kumarsambhav" has thus sung the glory of the Himalayas. The epic starts with the following verse :—

"Astuttrsyain dishi dewatatma Himalayoo nam nagadhirajah,

Purwaparoo toya nidhiwgahya sthitah prithbya ewa mandandah"

"In the north of Bharat, there is an emperor of the mountains named Himalaya. It is the soul of divinity. Extending from East to West it looks as a weighing scale to weigh the earth."

In Skanda Puran the Himalayas have been called the redeemer of all sins. A single thought of the Himalayas is greater than all the worships in Kashi. The glories of the Himalayas cannot be described in hundred divine years of the gods (which works out 432,000,000 years of this earth). A glance at the Himalayas can dry up all the sins.

Sages, poets and philosophers have sung the glory of Himalayas since ages. Himalayas, the temple of purity, have been telling man to grow pure like their snow peaks, which are beyond the reach of an atom of dust.

I continue watching the panorama, the glittering snow tops with a gigantic base of rugged rocks holding firmly the high peaks almost perpendicular. Far below are the green deodar, birch, oak and pine forests and down in the valley are deep gorges formed by the Alaknanda and the Dhauli rivers which come tumbling down from the high glaciers, tearing the hard rocks. The splendour, immensity and majesty all converge into a supernatural divinity. I perceive a mystic form of the Supreme Being in my heart and the great truth of Vedic seers comes to my mind; "all the elements and forms like fire, air, sun, moon and mountains are manifestations of the divine". To me Himalaya is a celestial temple where divinity is enshrined. I feel this divinity within, listen to its soft voice. Whispering in silence it says, "Oh man! From the beginning of creation I continue to bear the snow, the thunder, the sun, the rain and give you the life. I want nothing in return except that you should preserve me. Remember! Your life on this earth depends on my life."

My heart is full of happiness-happiness which the material world can never give. I bow to the Himalayas with absolute reverence and a thought comes to my mind, "Oh God! When just a fraction of your creation is so unique, so beautiful what must be the limit of your majesty, your beauty? Limitless, limitless, limitless, Neti, Neti, Neti.

2

Memories of School Days

Recapturing forgotten memories at the fag end of life is interesting and a fruitful pastime. Looking back I feel it was just yesterday that I was a youngster studying in lower classes at Nanital in the Thirties and then as a grown up in higher classes at Allahabad in early forties. The early years of my life were spent at Nanital. I had to walk a mile to reach my school at Mallital. School life was easy and interesting. There was no heavy load of the school bag as today. We carried a few books and notebooks in our hand and that made walking easy.

The memories of days spent with friends in this town with a beautiful lake are still fresh. There is a story behind this lake. In times long past, the inhabitants of this area considered the lake most sacred and did not reveal its whereabouts to any foreigner. During the year 1840 P. Baron an English trader and tourist was wandering in the Himalayas. He came to know about the lake and wanted to reach there. The local people misguided him. He understood their motive and played a trick. He employed some herdsmen to carry heavy load of stones and forced them to go on walking till they took him to the lake. The herdsmen got tired and had to take him to the lake to get rid of him.

Nar Singh, a landlord, was the owner of the lake and the surrounding area. Baron requested Nar Singh to sell the lake to him but he refused. Baron befriended him and invited him on a boat for a pleasure trip. When the boat reached the center of the lake Baron threatened to drown Nar Singh if he did not sign the sale deed. Needless to say, Nar Singh had to sign it and save his life.

Enchanted by the beauty and serenity of the lake and its surrounding hills covered with dense forests, the British, then a rising power, developed it into a hill station. It was made the summer capital of the then United Provinces of Agra and Awadh in the year 1857 and also the headquarters of the Eastern Command. The Englishmen established four residential colleges for their children, thus becoming a cosy home for British officers, the civil administration and army. They lived in luxury in spacious bungalows in picturesque spots on high hills. The government house has the most commanding sight on top of Tallital hill, covered with thick green forests.

After a circuitous journey on a winding road from Kathgodam as you reach the bus station you get the first view of the lake, which is a thrilling surprise. Gusts of cool wind welcome you and make you feel fresh. You feel a bundle of energy within. A stroll on the Mall Road along the right bank of the lake had its own pleasure. In those days it was a clean wide road with a gentle cover of small fine gravel, making it smooth for walking and safe for riding horses. The weeping willows planted along the bank added to the beauty of the lake and grandeur of the Mall. It is said, that in the old days Indians were not allowed to walk on the Mall. They used the small path below the Mall, close to the lake. In our times, however, there was no such restriction but the white domination was still there. Dressed in costly wollens the English men would walk or ride on their well-groomed horses like lords. Their ladies would go on palanquins (dandies in local dialect), which were carried by four men. They also enjoyed a ride in hand pulled rickshaws. Cars and other motor vehicles were not allowed to run on the Mall. Even the governor used to take his car very sparingly. There were just a few buildings along the mall and rarely a crowd even at the peak season.

Those were the days of civil disobedience. Mahatma Gandhi's name was on every lip. We considered him superhuman. I remember quite vividly one of his visits to Bhawali. It was the year 1928. I was eight year old. Gandhi ji came to address a meeting. The organizers had spread a bundle of khadi from the pandal to the point where Gandhi was to get down from his car and walk to the dais. Gandhi saw khadi and asked the organizers to roll it up at once. "Khadi is not to be spread like this and trampled upon".

The Englishmen treated Indians as inferiors and did not mix with them. At times the haughty, young school boys took sadistic pleasure in pulling down our caps, which was a great humiliation. I remember an unpleasant incident quite vividly even today.

One morning I was going to school with two of my friends. Trilochan was on my right. Near Y.M.C.A. on the Mall a British army officer came galloping on his horse. Suddenly his whip fell and he. asked Trilochan to pick it up. The freedom movement had infused a sense of self-respect and non-cooperation in us. Trilochan said, "Nahi uthayega" (I will not pick it up). This blunt reply infuriated the rider and he yelled in a hoarse voice, "Chokra jaldi uthayega "(boy pick it up quickly). Trilochan refused again.

The man dismounted from his horse, gave two slaps to Trilochan and made him pick up the whip. Thus ended Trilochan's experiment in civil disobedience. He was in tears. It is a sad incident and a reflection of those times.

There were two High Schools for Indian boys. A Government High School at Tallital, and the privately owned Chet Ram Sah Thulgharia High school at Mallital, where I studied. The teachers were gentle and took great interest in teaching. They were very cooperative and always ready to solve our problems. Though low paid they came well dressed. I specially remember Mr. Sinha. He was the most well dressed teacher. He taught us English and was very particular about cleanliness. Each day he would examine our hands, nails, hair and punish the boys who were not clean. Our teachers were our ideals.

I had many friends in school but Sunder Lal Sah was my most intimate friend. I cannot remember the moment we came close but from the first day we were one soul in two bodies, companions of several lives past. On the first day of the new session each year he would go to the next class and fix our seats together. We were together the whole day and met and played in the evening. Several incidents of our school life come to my mind. Padma Dutt Pant was our class teacher. He was the Mathematics teacher but taught us English as well. One day he gave an essay for homework. The next day he examined our copies, told the class that Sunder Lal had written the best essay and patted him. Sunder started weeping and said, "Sir it is not my work, my father helped me to write this" The teacher praised him all the more for disowning the false praise and speaking the truth.

A boy behind my seat was making a noise in the class. Padma Dutt mistook me for the boy, gave me a hard slap, and asked me to stand up. I stood up. "I never made any noise", I said, and started weeping He realized his mistake and after the interval came to the class with an apple.

"This apple I am going to give to the best boy in the class, who never makes a noise". He gave me the apple and went away. He used to feel sad whenever he had to punish the boys.

I was going to my class one day. Padma Dutt and Jagat Narayan our history teacher were following me. "This boy will get a first division this year" Padma Dutt said

"How can you say," Jagat Narayan asked. "Let us have a ten rupee bet".

I was listening to their conversation. I was in Tenth class then

Months after, one evening, I met Padma Dutt ji on the Mall road. I wished him.

"Here is a gift for you" he said "I have won the bet on account of your success and you deserve it". He put the ten rupee note in my pocket.

The sweet memory of our good teachers is fresh in my mind even today.

Our headmaster P. D. Sanwal was a strict disciplinarian. Fair and immaculately dressed in western style, he looked an Englishman. He had an imposing and awe-inspiring appearance. The students had a sense of fear. Punctually at 10 a. m. all the students would stand in class wise rows for prayer. After prayer he would give some sermons on good morals, truth etc. He would often relate the story of a boy who once asked his mother to give him some money to buy a pen. The mother refused. Next day he stole the pen of a fellow student and told his mother about it. The mother did not reprimand him. The boy took this as her approval and continued stealing things. As he grew up, he became a robber and murderer. When finally caught, he was tried and sentenced to death. He asked to see his mother as a last wish. When she came weeping and clasped her son, he bit her ear. The woman cried in pain and asked him the reason. The son said, "Mother, had you stopped me on the very first day I stole a pen I would not have to see this day."

Occasionally our headmaster would punish for misconduct naughty boys in the presence of other students. One day, he called Bachhi Singh of class seven and started caning him, initially on both the palms and then on the hips. We were stunned. During the interval we asked Bachi Singh as to what serious mischief he had done. He said he did nothing. Some students urged the head boy to meet the head master and inquire about the reason behind this severe punishment. The head master told the head boy that a girl student had complained to him that Bachhi Singh had teased her. Bachhi Singh denied the charge, when the boys asked him. We were enraged and decided to go on a strike; an uncommon and unheard of occurrence in those days. We boycotted classes the next day and assembled near Capitol cinema building on the Flat. The head master informed the Deputy Commissioner who was also chairman of the school management committee. The Deputy Commissioner came riding a horse and said in broken hindi, "Tum larka log school jayegee (you boys will go to the school). On our taking a firm stand he went away. At about one p. m. the head master sent the school chaukidar to warn us to come to the school at once or he would come with the stick. All the students ran to their classes like timid sheep. Such was the fear and sense of discipline which the teachers could instill among students.

I finished high school in the year 1938. The year was significant for our school as four students got first division, which was quite rare then. I was one of the lucky four. A high school certificate was valuable as it qualified one for entry into clerical and other subordinate government services, which was the lot of Indians during British Raj. Poverty and lack of resources prevented students from getting higher education and more than ninety percent of the boys ended their studies after high school.

I lived with my elder brother who was in government service in Nainital. There was a big age gap between us. He had great affection for me. I too had a great love, respect and regard for him. He took interest in my education and felt proud of my success and wanted me to join the best institution. Nainital had no intermediate college for Indian boys. The English schools catered mainly for the whites. In rare cases the wards of a few privileged, affluent and loyal families could get admission. I did not have that status but still my brother tried for my admission in St. Joseph's College on the basis of my merit but I could not get it.

Allahabad in those days was a reputed center of higher education. Many students from Nainital, Almora and Garhwal districts preferred to go there. My brother decided to send me to Allahabad. On 3rd of July 1938 I left for Lucknow with Sunder. His father was posted there. From Lucknow it was a lonely journey to Allahabad. The parting was most painful and in early months I cursed myself for not joining the college at Lucknow. I often ran to Lucknow on holidays and stayed with Sunder. His mother loved me as her own son and it was my sweet home. My mother was envious whenever I told her about her motherly love for me.

I reached Allahabad on 6th morning and asked the ekka wala (pony cart) to take me to some near-by hotel. He took me to a good hotel at Chowk. It was quite hot and I felt uncomfortable and lonely. Amar Kumar Mullick a close friend and class fellow at Nainital lived in Atarsuya Allahabad. In the evening I looked him up and was lucky to find him. I was to take admission in Government College but Mullick told me that Ewing Christian College was better, both for studies and extra curricular activities. We both got admission there on 8th July and were allotted single seated rooms in the hostel, a privilege at that time.

Far from the cool hills, into the hot and humid plains, I felt myself completely uprooted.

In the beginning we had to face some difficulties. Our classrooms were without fans and it was very hot and uncomfortable during summer and rains.

The constant running of trains over Yamuna Bridge caused a great disturbance. To top it all, the American teacher's pronunciation was difficult to follow-to say the least. Over time however, we got used to them.

Our Principal, C. M. Hazlett was a man of high principles. Once, the boys went on a strike. It is said that he still went to the class, gave his lecture to the empty class-even writing on the black board and came out; satisfied that he had done his duty.

An American lady who was the office superintendent would not pay the salary to peons and other low-grade employees unless they signed. She would not accept thumb impression, as was the common practice. This forced the employees to learn writing their name. This was her novel literacy campaign.

As time passed I got busy with classes and a new circle of friends. There were a good number of students from the hills and we spent our evenings together. Ragging by senior students was the lot of the fresher but it all passed off well.

We had all types of games in the evening. Swimming was compulsory for 1st year students for a month. Mr. Gideon our game's teacher was very particular about it and said it was the best exercise. He used to relate the story of a philosopher who went out for boating on a full moon night. The beauty of the moon and its reflection in the water enchanted him

"Do you enjoy this beauty, boatman?"

"No", said the boatman.

"You have lost half the charm of your life, boatman."

Suddenly there was a storm.

"Philosopher, do you know how to swim?"

"No boatman."

"You have lost the whole charm of your life" said the boatman.

I was interested in swimming and boating. I learnt swimming and joined the college boat club. Yamuna was then a clean river with blue waters and we enjoyed diving into it and at times crossed it. On holidays we went out for boating up to 'Sangam'. The return was tough especially if the wind was against us.

The most interesting and educative part of our college life was the Thursday assembly. Prominent celebrities of the day were invited to address the students in the Tooker Hall facing river Yamuna. Those were the days of the freedom movement. Allahabad being the headquarters of the Indian National Congress was the hub of political activity. Eminent freedom fighters and leaders who visited the town were invited. We had the privilege of listening to Pt. Jawaharlal Nehru several times. He being the resident of Allahabad was available and was very kind to oblige whenever students made a request. We heard Netaji Subhas Chandra Bose, Sardar Patel, Dr. Radhakrishnan, Bhula Bhai Desai, Pt. Sunder Lal, Pt. Govind Ballab Pant and many academicians. The most memorable visit was that of Netaji Bose. A tall, fair and handsome person with a radiant face he was a unique personality. There was a big gathering hence arrangements were made in the open ground. A prominent girl student was to garland Netaji on his arrival. The loud speaker was playing nationalistic songs. Some boys who were handling the gramophone put the song of a recent movie Vidyapati. As Netaji arrived and the girl was garlanding him, the first line of the song, "Anuradha what have you done? "You have garlanded me," was in the air. Netaji gave a hearty laugh. The boys clapped and the slogan of Netaji Subhas Chandra Bose zindabad resounded in the air. Netaji went on to give a thunderous speech.

Another of his visits in 1941 was still more memorable. Due to serious differences with Gandhiji and Congress, Netaji had left the party and formed the "Forward Block". He came on a visit to Allahabad. We went to see him at the railway station. There was a big crowd of students as well as members of the new party. The president of the party was there to receive him. Bose was profusely garlanded as he came out of the station. He was to be the guest of Dr. Banerjee of Allahabad University. As he was being escorted to his car, Pt. Nehru arrived. Both wished each other. "How can it be?" Pt Nehru said. "You have to came and stay with me". Ideologies and alliances were forgotten at a glance. Both shook hands and went together to Anand Bhawan. That was the greatness of the two. One can never think of such relationships today. Bose was to address a public meeting in Tandon Park in the evening. Pt. Nehru brought him in his car, dropped him near the Park and waited for him on the roadside. He took him back after the speech was over. The city president of Forward Block, an old freedom fighter said that he had never seen such a huge crowd in Allahabad during his long life.

My first year in college was excellent. Busy in studies, games, boating and swimming and attending the speeches of the great men of the day, I did not know how the year passed.

3

The Mortal Cut

It was July 1939. The College reopened after summer vacations and we moved to a new hostel meant for senior boys. Four of us who lived in adjacent rooms pooled in pans, saucers and a stove to organize a 'tea club' where we had much needed breaks in course of the daily studies. In December a hostel mate Haldhar Prasad Nigam joined our tea club. There are faces that attract and impress you at first sight while there are others who give little or no response. Nigam was in the latter category and did not impress me at our first meeting. He was stout, with a round face and long hair. A carefree type, he was not much interested in studies.

It was early March 1940 and we were neck deep in preparations for the final board examinations. Suddenly riots broke out in the city and curfew was imposed. Normal life was completely disrupted. One evening I felt my body aching. By night I was running high fever. I dragged myself to the college dispensary the next morning and got some medicines. The fever however continued. There was just a week left for the examinations and I become nervous. All my friends were busy in their studies and had little or no time for me. With fever lingering on I felt weak and knew not what to do.

On the third day of my illness as I lay on the bed in fever and pain, there was a knock at the door.

"Come in", I said.

It was Nigam. I was a bit surprised for it was the first time he had come to my room.

"Please sit down".

"I have just heard that you are ill. How are you now? Did you take any medicine?"

"Yes, I did, but there's no relief. I am worried. How will I appear in the examinations?"

"You need to see some good physician in the city", Nigam said. "Dr. Banerjee is the best one. Let us go to him"' he emphasized.

"There is rioting in the city" I said. "It is not possible to move out".

"I know a tongawala", Nigam replied. "I often hire him. I am just going to request him to take us to Dr Banerjee in the city."

He asked me to get ready and left my room abruptly without waiting for my consent. He probably felt it unnecessary. His words struck me. There was no other way and I got ready.

Nigam was back in half an hour with the tonga. I came out and locked the room. Nigam helped me down the stairs and got me seated comfortably in the tonga.

The tongawala, a fairly aged person drove us through unfrequented and safe by lanes. The whole place bore a completely deserted look. Soon we were at the door of Dr. Banerjee's house. Nigam knocked the door.

"Who is there?" Someone asked from inside.

"We are students from Ewing Christian College" Nigam said. "My friend is ill and we want to see Dr. Banerjee."

Dr. Banerjee, an old man came near the door and peeped through a hole. After ascertaining that we were students and in need of medical aid the doctor opened the door.

"How could you dare to come here in this riot?" he said.

"I am having high fever for the last three days", I said. "My final examinations are about to start and if I do not get well I will lose a year."

"Lose a year! You could have lost your life. Come in"! He offered us chairs, examined me thoroughly and gave me some tablets and a bottle of liquid mixture.

"Take it after every six hours" he said. "God willing you will be fit in a day or two". I offered him his fees but he declined. "Take care and go safely", he said, and waved his hand. I bowed and said, "Sir I have no words to express my gratitude."

The tongawala brought us back safely to the hostel. Nigam accompanied me to my room. When we were seated I took hold of his hand and said, "How shall I thank you

Nigam for all that you have done for me. You took such a bold step and risked your own life for me when none of my close friends were of any help. I was never close to you but still you came out bravely. I will never forget this in my life." He gave me a rare smile, stood up and left the room".

Since that day Nigam became my best friend. Dr. Banerjee's medicine cured me in a day. Though weak I was fit to appear in the examination and we both passed.

We joined the Allahabad University in July 1940. I got a good room in Holland Hall hostel, a unit of the Allahabad Christian College, the other being the Ewing Christian College and Naini Agriculture College. Nigam was a day scholar and lived with some relatives in Dara Ganj. He was a regular visitor to my room and we spent most of our evenings together with some other friends. I did my Bachelor's degree in arts in 1942 but Nigam failed to qualify in the Bachelor's degree in science.

In July 1942 I joined law classes. Nigam started living in a rented room with his elder brother who came to join the University. In August 1942 Mahatma Gandhi started the Quit India movement. On August 4th or 5th Pt. Nehru gave a rousing speech at Alfred park in civil lines asking all the Indians to give a last blow to the British Raj and get India's freedom. There was lot of enthusiasm among the students. No one attended classes. Huge processions were taken out from the Union building of the University. I along with Nigam and other friends joined the procession which took a round of the civil lines area. Loud cries of slogans and Bandey Matram were heard from distances far away. One day the students resolved to hoist the tricolor flag on the collectorate building. A big police force came and tried to disperse the crowd. There was a lathi charge but the students stood firm. Firing was ordered and a brave boy, Lal Padma Dhar Singh who was asking the students to lie down, was himself shot dead. The crowd became furious and unruly. The news of the firing and death of Lal Padma Dhar Singh spread like wild fire. People came out and started damaging public property. The situation became uncontrollable. The administration imposed a curfew and the Army was called out. The message of Gandhi's call to the British to quit India spread throughout the country and the nation was in turmoil. All the top leaders were arrested and shifted to unknown places. The University was closed for an indefinite period. Students were virtually driven out of the hostels. All the hostel messes were closed and even the restaurants were ordered not to serve any food, tea etc. We had no option but to leave for our homes. Nigam and I went together up to Lucknow from where he parted for Unnao and I left for Nainital.

The University reopened in December 1942 after four months. Regular classes were resumed. Summer vacations came and we were preparing to go to our homes. One evening Nigam came to my room and asked me to accompany him to some booksellers. He wanted to purchase some books for the vacations. We went to the market. I selected some novels by Thomas Hardy and Nigam purchased the famous book on palmistry "The Language of the Hand" by Cheiro.

We were back in the university in July 1943. Nigam was now living in a rented room with his elder brother near Prayag Station. Pandey, a freedom fighter and a social worker had opened a restaurant in Colonel Ganj.

He was very friendly with Nigam. Most of the students had patronized his restaurant where we often met for tea or dinner. Nigam met me there one evening.

"Hello", I said, "How did you spend your vacations, what about the book on palmistry? You must have studied it and become a master palmist." I stretched my palm and asked him to foretell my future.

He came closer, pressed my palm and looking through his gloomy eyes said, "Yes, I did study the book thoroughly and compared my palm". He stopped and looked in the other direction.

"And what did you find?"

"It is better you do not ask me further".

"Don't keep me in suspense; tell me what was there in the book!".

He released my palm and withdrew with a sigh. He looked tense and dejected.

"I will tell you later", he said in a feeble voice.

I watched him closely. He was different. I found him withdrawn as if something mysterious was haunting him and preventing him to reveal. Seeing him upset I did not press further and dismissed it as a figment of his fantasies.

"Forget it", I said with a smile. "Let us have a cup of tea." To cheer him up I started some other topic of the day. A few friends joined us and we parted after the tea.

Nigam came to my room every evening but I found him somewhat different. He talked little and was not as cheerful as he used to be. I had a fear that the ghost of the palmist was working imperceptibly in his mind. It was the month of September. Rains had ceased and the weather was pleasant He did not come for two evenings consecutively. I felt worried and went to his room. To my surprise he was lying on his bed. I touched his arm. He had high fever.

"This fever is going to take my life" He said.

"Why did you not inform me?". I asked his brother to bring a tonga to take him to the University dispensary. We got him admitted in the dispensary ward. The doctor examined him and gave medicine. I stayed with him till late night.

The next day I went to see him at about 2 p. m. The door of his room was half open and I saw him examining his palm very closely. As I entered the room he put his hand behind his neck and gave me a fake smile. I sat near him and inquired about his fever.

"I am better now", he said, "The doctor has allowed me to go back to my room."

"Why are you so obsessed about your palm?" I asked, "Take a positive view of life and forget whatever you have read." I brought a tonga and took him to his room.

He limited his visits to my room so I went to him every now and then. The long Deshera vacations neared. Suresh Pant my close friend in K. G. Medical College at Lucknow urged me to spend the holidays with him. One evening I went to Nigam and asked if he would accompany me to Lucknow.

"I am staying here to study to get through this year," he said. I did not press the matter and left for Lucknow. I had a nice time with Pant and his friends. After three days of my stay I got a letter from Nigam saying he again had the fever and was going home to Unnao with his brother. He asked me to meet him at Lucknow Railway Station. I received Nigam at the Railway Station the next morning. His face was pale and he looked depressed.

"How are you now?" I asked.

"So, so" he said, and avoided my looks.

He had grown weak. I put him on the train to Unnao.

"Sit down with me" he said, "Promise that you will come to my house the day after."

"Well", I said, "You will get well soon and you should come to Lucknow. We will spend our holidays here together."

"That has to be seen", he said, and stressed, "You have to come."

"I will definitely come" I assured him

The train was about to leave. I got down. He gave me a very pathetic look, which moved me. I left with a heavy heart.

As promised I left for Unnao the third day. I was passing through Kaisarbagh when, my closest friend Sunder who happened to be there spotted me. He was with his cousin.

"Where are you going? When did you come? Why did you not come to my house?" He flung a volley of questions at me. I used to stay with him whenever I dropped at Luchnow and this was the first time that I stayed with Pant. Sunder seemed annoyed. I tried to pacify him and said that I was in a hurry to go to Unnao to see Nigam who was ill and would surely come to him on return. His cousin invited me for a cold drink. He took me to a shop and offered a glass of some drink followed by sweets. We walked up to Aminabad from where I was to take a rickshaw. As I walked a few steps my head started reeling and I felt a strange sensation all over my body. My feet were trembling.

"What was it that you offered to me?" I asked.

"It was bhang" (hemp), I was told.

The bhang intoxicated me and it was not possible for me to go to Railway Station. In the mean time another friend K. P. Dabral met us and they all took me to Sunder's house at Nazarbagh. My condition started deteriorating and all were worried. I was given butter to enable me to vomit but nothing came out. I felt uneasy and my body was burning. After taking a long shower, I went to sleep under a fan. Dabral was by my side. I was now feeling a little better. I drifted into an uneasy sleep, only to be rudely awakened. I had a dream that Nigam had passed away. I was shocked and told Dabral about the dream with tears in my eyes. Dabral tried to pacify me saying it was only a dream.

Early next morning I felt refreshed. "I must go now", I said. My friend told me that the train for Unnao would leave at ten and I should go after meals. Curry and rice was ready. Just after taking my meal I again started feeling dizzy and was unable to stand. The journey to Unnao was thus put off.

The next day I was quite normal. I boarded the train to Unnao at ten in the morning. It pulled out of the station and I watched the countryside pass by. The train seemed to be running slow or was it my impatience that made the journey seem long? My mind was drawing up different images. Nigam may be much better now, I thought. It was now five days since I had seen him last. I was feeling guilty for not keeping the promise but circumstances had made me helpless. "I will tell him the whole story. How I was offered a drink that made me sick. He would be convinced. He may be fit to accompany me to Lucknow." I was lost in these musings when I found that the train had reached Unnao station. I reached Nigam's house, which was at a walking distance. There was no one outside. I knocked the door; Nigam's elder brother came out.

"How is Nigam? Take me to his room please". I asked in all eagerness.

"Where shall I take you brother? He is gone. You are too late." He came close and clasped me in his arms. He was weeping.

His words shattered my mind. The images I had drawn were broken into pieces. I was stunned.

"I can't believe it. Tell me how and when it all happened", I said in a choked voice.

He took me inside and sat near me.

"Haldhar waited for you the whole day. You had promised to come. He had never asked mother to cook any thing special but that day he requested her to prepare food of your choice. He knew your taste. His eyes were towards the door. He lost hope in the evening and asked me to give a pen and paper. He wrote something and kept the paper below his pillow. Some hours before his death, he gave me that paper".

"Give this to my friend whenever you meet him", he told me in a feeble voice. He died at about one in the morning.

Strange! It was the hour when I had the dream of his passing away.

He went inside, brought a folded paper and gave it to me.

I opened it with trembling fingers. The following lines were scribbled in an irregular hand.

"I did not reveal to you then. The day has come to tell you. I have a mortal cut in my palm. I knew I would not live. I waited for you. You did not come."

The words pierced my heart. I felt suffocated and wept bitterly.

Nigam's father and mother heard my cries. They came, sat close to me and tried to console. Their grief was much greater than mine. They had lost their young son.

"He was very keen to see you," said his father.

"He asked me to prepare so many dishes", wailed his mother.

How could I tell them the role destiny had played with me? I stayed with the bereaved family till evening and came back to Lucknow.

As I reflect back, his gloomy face at Pandey's restaurant and his sad, distressed looks at Lucknow railway station flash before my eyes. They were the imperceptible signals of the coming event, which I had brushed aside. How sure he was about the end, his conviction on the mortal cut, which he concealed from me then and revealed by scratching on paper while nearing his end. I wanted him to forget it over a cup of tea. How could he have erased that mortal cut which had gone deep down his mind?

Could he have been saved? Why did I not take him to Dr. Banerjee as he had taken me risking his life on that fateful day? Why the thought did not occur to either of us? Why was I obstructed on my way to see him? Why should he have loved me so much?

All these questions haunted me for long and I found no answer.

4

Early Years of Community Development

Transfer from Bijnor, a small town, to Meerut the best town of western U. P. in December 1950 was a welcome change. I was working in the Department of Economics and Statistics. The charter of my duties included collection of data for economic surveys of rural and urban areas, reporting weekly wholesale and retail prices of food grains and essential commodities from different markets of the district and conducting miscellaneous economic surveys.

I had my office and residence in Abu lane near Sadar Bazar in Meerut. It was a mansion with a big compound and an orchard and was also shared by the house owner and a Sardarji who was once a well to do lawyer in Rawalpindi but now a refugee. We lived like a family. I had nice neighbors and a circle of good friends. My daughter was in a good school. Life was smooth and comfortable.

In March 1954 my nephew who was studying law showed me an advertisement about the recruitment of 30 posts of block development officers in the Community Development Department of the U. P. Government and wanted me to type his application for the post. Even as I did it, the grade and pay scale for this post tempted me and I also sent an application though half-heartedly.

I was called for an interview at Lucknow in early June. There were hundreds of candidates and the competition was very tough. Most of the candidates were weeded out in the preliminary board. I got through and appeared in the final board next morning. Shri A N Jha I. C. S., Development Commissioner and the most important member of the board asked me several questions about rural and urban unemployment, landless labour, interest rates, rural industries and crop rotation patterns. Since I had worked in this field my replies were correct and to the point. I came out optimistic but still sceptic.

It was a surprise when after a month I got intimation from my department that I was selected and should report to the Principal "Bakshi ka Talab" training center at Lucknow for training in the first week of August. I was now in a fix. I knew nothing about the department, its working and place of posting. So far I was playing with my whims and was neither serious nor hopeful about my selection. A friend told me that the department was created for the development of rural areas and I would have to live and work in the remote areas. Well settled in a city like Meerut, this meant a complete dislocation of my family and education of my children. The temptation of a higher pay scale that had prompted me to apply vanished.

In the evening I went to see S.C. Misra, a friend who lived close to my house. As chance would have it one of his acquaintances, who was also selected as Block Development Officer, had come to see him. He had a better knowledge about the department and its working. I requested him to explain to me the set-up of the department, its working and prospects. He told me that each district had been divided into a number of blocks smaller than a tehsil to serve as an administrative unit for all round development of that area. The block is under the charge of a Block Development Officer, who coordinated the activities of all the development departments like agriculture, horticulture, animal husbandry, cooperative and public health. He had to put into effect the sanctioned village plans and projects. Some blocks had started functioning and others were to be opened in a phased manner. In due course the whole country was to be covered. It was thus going to be a very big organization. Pt Nehru, the Prime Minister was personally interested in this gigantic programme.

The rosy picture drawn by him inspired me. I compared it to my present job. Here I was collecting data from irresponsive samples, a dull routine work. I did not have job satisfaction and often craved for a change. This was an opportunity, a new opening in life. I could take initiative and work for the betterment of the villages besides getting a better grade and pay. Misra encouraged me. I decided to join the new department. I handed over charge to my reliever and left my family with my youngest brother who was Veterinary Surgeon at Roorkee. I left for Lucknow the next morning.

At Lucknow I met J. K. Pandey Director of Economics and Statistics. He congratulated me and said that I was now joining a more responsible post and expected me to work hard.

I joined Bakshi Ka Talab Training center on 7th July 1954. Initially 30 candidates were selected but since a number of blocks were to be opened in near future, 102 candidates were called for training as per merit list. The training center was functioning in old buildings of the Air Force built during the Second World War. We were accommodated in spacious barracks. The trainees ran a common mess. We were required to wash our own dishes. The center had a dress code of khaki shirt, khaki half pant and a white Gandhi cap. We had to be ready by six in the morning. After physical training, tea and breakfast, classes were held to give us lessons in agriculture, horticulture, animal husbandry, cooperative, public health, and social education by experts in these fields. Occasionally the Development Commissioner and the Deputy Development Commissioners lectured on various programmes and our duties in the field. We were taken to neighboring villages to acquaint ourselves with the ongoing development programmes and run adult literacy classes at night.

The trainees gave cultural performances such as folk dances, folk songs, short plays. The overall assessment of the trainees included their performance in cultural programmes besides the class and fieldwork. There was a race to put up the best show.

We were trained in various methods of extension such as audio visual aids, posters, puppet shows, short plays and direct talks and contact with the villagers. There was emphasis to shed the urban sophisticated mentality and be one with the village folk to gain their confidence. The basic idea of rendering extension service to the farmers was borrowed from America where this service existed in each county. Farmers were enlightened about improved methods of farming, dairy, cattle breeding, horticulture etc. It meant extending expertise to the doorstep of the farmer. In the year 1952 the scheme was experimented in Mohoba Project in Etawa district of U. P. Albert Mayer an American expert was invited by the government as adviser. Sri D. P. Singh an efficient officer of administrative service was the chief coordinator of the project. The scheme was a success and was given wide publicity through newspapers and documentaries on the screen. Community Projects were opened in each district on this pattern. Subsequently their size was reduced and National Extension Service Blocks were opened in phases in each district.

Our training was completed in November 1954. We were attached to the functioning blocks in our home districts till the opening of new blocks in January 1955. Three of us, belonging to Garhwal district, opted for Dhangu block in Garhwal district. Here we came in touch with practical working in the field. We visited the villages and worked with the field staff. Those were the initial days and there was great enthusiasm, both among the staff and the people. Self help and shramdan (voluntary labour) were the slogans of the day. Construction of bridle paths and motor roads was taken up by the gram sabhas (village councils) with their own labour. The Satpuli-Naugaonkhal motor road in Chaundkot Pargana of Garhwal is a unique example of people's voluntary efforts and determination. A motor road from Gumkhal to Silogi in Dhangu block was taken up in December 1954. Villagers came in large number with their implements. We participated in the project and it was a great experience. This reminds me of the spirit of mutual cooperation and community life that existed in our villages in good old days. People came forward to help each other in the construction of houses, transporting timber and slates, planting paddy, construction and repair of irrigation channels and roads. That spirit of community life has disappeared now. People bank on government for even small things. Man is confined to himself and his family.

In this context I remember a song sung by the Principal and the trainees in the training center. An extension teacher composed the song. I render here its English translation.

Create a World Anew

Oh mighty son of mighty soil!

Bring heaven on earth with your own toil.

With courage and your own resource,

With body, mind and a pious soul,

Fill fresh life in bodies of villages outworn.

Shed ideas decayed, outdated, outworn.

Create a world anew; be bold.

In the second week of January 1955 I received my posting order as Block Development Officer of Salt Block in district Almora. Though a resident of hills I had never heard the name of the place "Salt". The posting did not appeal to me but there was no choice. I left for Almora on 22 Dec. and reached there on 23rd evening. Almora is an old town at an altitude height of 1646 meters. Spread over a long ridge, the city looks beautiful from distant hills. It was the capital of Kumaon during the long reign of Chand dynasty. King Balo Kalyan Chand shifted the capital from Champawat to Almora in the year 1563 because of its central location. After ridding Uttarakhand of the Gurkha regime in 1815, the East India Company made it the headquarters of the Divisional Commissioner of Kumaon.

I met M. S. Chand, the District Planning Officer, told him about my posting as Block Development Officer of

Salt block and inquired about its location and the headquarter. Chand consulted the file but the headquarter was not mentioned there. He made inquires from the Assistant Collector Ranikhet but he too had no knowledge. He then contacted H. G. Pant Deputy Speaker and M. L. A. of the area. Pant told him that he was to inaugurate the block at Shahid Smarak (Martyr Memorial, village Khumarh) in Salt Patti. He however did not know about the, headquarter. Chand asked me to proceed to Khumarh; its location was still a mystery. As I was leaving, I met two young men. They introduced themselves as Prem Chand Pandey and Hira Ballav Tiwary and said that they were posted as Village Level Workers in Salt block and wanted to accompany me to the block. I felt a sense of relief that I now had some company. I asked them to meet me at the bus station at 8 the next morning.

It was snowing when we left for Ranikhet on 25th morning. We reached Ranikhet at ten thirty. It was still snowing. We went to a hotel and warmed ourselves near a fireplace. After a hot cup of tea I asked my companions to find out the route to Khumarh. They returned after half an hour and told me that we had to go to Mohan on Ranikhet-Ramnagar road and change the bus for Sankar. From Sankar Khumarh was about 10 miles, nearly three quarters of a day on foot.

We left for Mohan in the afternoon and reached late in the evening. After dropping us at bus station the bus left for Ramnagar. Mohan was a lonely place in the valley. There was a hut on the right side of the road, the front portion of which had a tea stall and a provision store and at the rear a few cots were laid. We stayed in the hut. It was drizzling and dark. I could see some tall trees in the dim light of the lamp. My companions cooked the meal and we had a good rest after the day's journey.

The morning was clear and sunny. I took a small round of the area. Amid dense forest Mohan was then a small place with a forest rest house some distance above the motor road. I had read about this rest house in Jim Corbett's book "The Man Eaters of Kumaon". Corbett had stayed here when he had come to kill a man-eater. There are some residential houses of the officials of the forest department on a ridge across the road. These forests once abounded in wild animals and birds. Indiscriminate hunting during the British rule and even for years after independence resulted in large-scale destruction of wild life. Hunting was the privilege of bureaucrats and rajas. There were good hunters even among local people. I remember, once while coming from Sankar to Mohan, a hunter climbed up the roof of the bus after requesting the driver to stop the bus on hearing the gun shot. He shot several fowls and hares within a short distance and shared them with the driver. The government slept over such indiscriminate destruction for many years and opened its eyes when the major damage had been done. A forest area of 1319 square kilometers was declared a national sanctuary and named Corbett National Park after the name of Jim Corbett, the famous hunter who killed many man-eaters and saved several human lives. You have now to roam several miles on the back of an elephant and try your luck for a glimpse of the king of the forest in an area which once resounded with the roar of tigers.

The bus from Ramnagar to Sankar reached Mohan at nine in the morning. It was full of passengers for Salt area. Many residents of Salt own land and houses in villages around Ramnagar and migrate there during winter. Situated near the foot hills on the right bank of the river Kosi, Ramnagar is the main market for Salt area and villages falling in Dhumakot and Bajoron region of

Garhwal district. It also caters for villages on the Ramnagar-Ranikhet motor road in Nainital district. Ramnagar was named after Sir Henry Ramsay, the commissioner of Kumaon from 1856 to 1884; a long period of 28 years. It was connected with Moradabad by a narrow gauge railway line in 1907.

The villagers were coming to witness the opening ceremony of the block, which was a great event in those days. I boarded the bus and took a seat. On learning that I was the Block Development Officer of their block they offered me the front seat occupied by Diwan Singh, Pradhan of Pokhri Gram Sabha. Front seat used to be the privilege of officials or local leaders.

We reached Sanker at eleven. It was a small place with a few shops. Diwan Singh who by now had become quite familiar with me took over as my host and guide. He arranged for a mule for transporting our luggage and we started our march. After crossing the river Ramganga, we reached Marchula. The road bifurcates from here to Baijro in Garhwal district and to Manila in Almora district. We took the Manila road to the right. We had to cross a river called Badangad on which there was no bridge. During rains the river used to be in spate and some people were washed away every year while crossing. I remember once I had to stay at Marchula for two days to wait for the water to recede and could cross it only with the help of two strong swimmers. After climbing over the barren hills and covering a distance of eight miles, Diwan Singh took us to his village Talli Pokhari. The whole area was absolutely bleak, dreary and cheerless. I felt profoundly depressed and out of place. Diwan Singh accommodated me in his drawing room, which was quite clean. He invited us for dinner that night and served delicious dishes, which he said, was the custom of the village. From the next day we had our separate kitchen. His hospitality made me feel at home in that unfamiliar land.

The next day we went to Khumarh to help local people in making arrangements for the opening day. Khumarh is a small village on the eastern side of the hill, about one kilometer from the main road. The four patties of Salt and neighboring areas, I was told, played an important role in the freedom struggle since 1921. They took active part in the noncooperation movement and stopping coolie begar (forced labour). They started spinning on spinning wheels and wearing khadi clothes (hand spun and hand woven) and introduced many reforms such as non-smoking, keeping the village clean and ensuring clean drinking water.

In August 1942, Gandhi who was fighting a long nonviolent war for independence of India delivered an ultimatum to British rulers to quit India. It was known as Quit India Movement. There was a big uprising in Salt area during this movement of 1942. Johnson, the Assistant Collector Ranikhet came with a big police force to suppress the rising. He arrested many people. They were beaten with sticks and rifle butts. A huge crowd had gathered at Khumar to protest against this tyranny. Johnson ordered firing and four freedom fighters lost their lives. A Memorial was subsequently erected near the village in memory of the martyrs.

Quite a number of people had gathered at the Memorial to decorate it with festoons and make a dais. I was introduced to the local leaders, prominent being Laxman Singh Adhikari who was once a teacher but resigned and took an active part in the struggle for freedom. He became M. L. A. after some years and vacated his seat for C. B. Gupta Chief Minister of UP, who was defeated in his Lucknow constituency. The other was Raghubar Dutt Upadhay, a freedom fighter.

In the evening Har Govind Pant Deputy Speaker reached with M. S. Chand D. P. O. and S. P. Mukarjee(I. A. S.) Assistant Collector Ranikhet. They stayed in the primary and middle school buildings.

It was 28th January 1955, the day of inauguration of the block. The day was clear but windy. The recent rains had brought down the temperature.

Salt block is comprised of five patties, four patties of Salt namely, Talla, Malla, Walla and Palla Salt and Walla Naya, with a total area of about 3,000 sq miles. Its boundary meets that of district Garhwal on the West and district Nanital on the South.

There was a very good gathering at Khumar. People from distant and neighboring villages started arriving in the forenoon. They were well dressed, most of them in khadi clothes with white Gandhi caps. A good number of ladies had come in their bright local dresses of ghagra (big long skirts) and pichora (long scarfs) and jewelry. The whole arena bore a festive look.

H. G. Pant, the chief guest arrived at two in the afternoon. He was received with the beating of drums and blowing of *ransing* (big local trumpet), garlanded and led to the dais, which was full with local leaders. A microphone was specially hired from Ramnagar for the occasion. Every leader wanted to speak and some made lengthy speeches, heralding a new era and anticipated the fulfillment of long dreams for the development of their backward area. The long list of speakers was cut short and the chief guest was requested to address the audience. H. G. Pant urged the people to come together and work hard to eradicate poverty. "The government", he said, "Would do its best to provide financial help through the agency of the block". He inaugurated the block.

We were now in search of a suitable place and building for the block office. Nandan Singh a resident of village Malli Pokhary offered his new double story house on rent. Situated on the top of a hill, Malli Pokhary was a small village on the main Marchula Manila road near Khumarh. Located in the middle of the village the house was unsuitable but there was no other house available. Chand the District-Planning Officer approved it and the house was hired on rent.

Chand advised me to go to Tarikhet block which had started a few years back and collect information about the approved firms for the purchase of equipments for office and other schemes. He said I should come to Almora to recruit office staff. He left for Almora the same day.

Left with the two Village Level Workers in Diwan Sngh's house, I was reminded of my days at Meerut. "What a change in life?", I thought. I felt lonely and depressed but it was necessary for me to adjust to the new environment to enable me to shoulder the responsibility of establishing a new office and start work in the field with courage and fortitude.

Diwan Singh's house was inconvenient as it was down in the valley. I had to climb up to reach my office. Luckily I got a spacious house at Kathalkot, a village with a few dewellings on top of a hill near Debayal, about a kilometer from my office. Debayal had a primary school, junior high school, dispensary and a shop. I shifted to this house.

A visit to Tarikhet block enabled me to collect information about the approved firms. I placed orders for furniture and other requirements for the office. My next trip was to Almora to get my office staff members. N. B. Joshi, an experienced accountant of planning office was selected as the head clerk cum accountant. Laxmi Lal Sah and Diwan Singh were new entrants for the post of typist and storekeeper. Four messengers were recruited. On my return I visited the Haldwani Furnerture Mart, checked the furniture and got it dispatched to the block office. A transport agency was established at Sanker, the motor head, to receive goods from Ramnagar railway station for onward dispatch to the block.

The staff started joining their duties and was accommodated in the house I lived, till they could find suitable rooms in villages nearby. We started a common mess. We faced problems in that remote area and a community life was the only answer. We lived like a family.

It was now one and half month. Despite all my efforts I could not adjust myself. I was worried about my wife and children who were at Roorkee. The education of my daughter was suffering.

I went to Roorkee to bring my luggage. My wife insisted to accompany me. She was in the family way. I told her that there was no medical facility in that area and it would be an unwise step. My elder brother was settled in Haldwani, which was nearer. I told her that it would be more convenient for me to look after them if she agreed to stay at Haldwani for the present. She would get all the medical help there, but she was insistent and accompanied me. She was more worried about me than herself.

We reached Sanker from where we had to walk on foot to Debayal. My wife walked about two miles with great difficulty and was quite unable to walk. We spent the night in a small room in a village nearby and reached Debayal the next morning.

M. D. Joshi a compounder in the local dispensary lived with his family next door. His wife acquainted my wife with the difficulties they were facing. She told her that there was neither any medical aid nor any experienced woman to help at childbirth. My wife now realized the situation and agreed to move to Haldwani.

After a brief time with my family I was lonely again. I was worried about my wife who suffered during her previous confinements She needed care. My children had been missing me all these months. Moving from place to place they felt disturbed and uncomfortable. It hurt me. My daughter could not join any school since we left Meerut and son was of school going age. I had thought of giving them good education in a decent school. This was a remote possibility now. Meanwhile I received an offer of a promotion in my parent department. I thought of reverting back but that would defeat the very purpose of my joining this post. I had come to the new department with an aim and mission. I wanted to devote myself to development work in villages. Besides this, my brother who had helped and encouraged me in my education had high hopes and had wished that I should try and get into the provincial civil service which otherwise I could not. During my last meeting he told me that I had now a chance to become District-Planning Officer, a post held by senior P. C. S. officers. "He was keen to see that day", he said. Dislocation of my family life and posting in this remote barren area, however, dampened my determination and my brother's dream. I found myself in a conflict, a duality that agitated my mind and made me restless. I could not sleep.

Dejected, worried and sad I went for a long walk one evening. I climbed up a hill, sat on a cozy spot from where I could see several villages on both sides of the hill and the distant mountains and river Ramganga down below. The cattle were returning home, half starved after roaming over the barren hills with scanty grass here and there. There were good rains this winter and fields were green with a good wheat crop. The farmers had ploughed some of their fallow land for the coming summer crops. There was still some time for the sun to set and it was absolutely calm. Suddenly my eyes fell on a village where a grim tragedy occurred a few days earlier. An old widow had three sons. Two of them lived with her in the village and the third worked down in the plains. He was returning home after a long time. His two brothers went to the bus stand to receive him and help him carry his luggage. As they climbed the hill there was a sudden hailstorm. They ran to take shelter under a tree. Lightning struck the tree and took away their lives. What a tragic fate? Three young lives lost in a second and what a terrible tragedy for the unfortunate widow? She lost every thing in this miserable world. I thought of her and. forgot my own worries, which stood nowhere. An inner voice said, “Lighten other’s burden and you lighten your own”. I tried to still my mind and let the inner self speak. “Do not live in duality”, it said. “Duality leads to depression and frustration. Be firm”, it added, “there should be no deviation in your former determination to serve the villages, the people, the area you have been sent, but remember you can only serve the area and the people if you love them and the place where they live.” I loved the people who were simple, innocent and poor. I loved my staff and the staff had great love and respect for me. Let me cultivate love for this remote barren area as well I thought. A return would be a shameful retreat. I decided to plunge myself to the task allotted by the invisible power; the ultimate decision maker.

I chalked out my programme. I first went to Lucknow to place orders with the approved firms for the purchase of different articles. I pressed them to dispatch the goods at earliest as the budget was to be utilized by 31st March. I then made a long tour of the block. Wherever I went the villagers gathered in good number. They welcomed me and put forward their problems. The biggest problem in the block was of drinking water, which was given top priority. The next was of fuel and fodder. Poor ladies had to walk miles to fetch water and fuel for the hearth and fodder for their cattle. The surrounding hilltops were barren hence planting forests was the next priority. There was then a demand for repair of school buildings and opening of new schools. I asked the field staff to get resolutions from the gram sabhas (village councils) prepare plan and estimates and send them to me.

Work in the field and office started with speed. The whole day we were busy in office or in the field but the evenings were very dull. There was neither company nor entertainment. I was interested in music since my younger days. I thought of organizing a music group. I was told that there were some good bhajan mandlies (group singers) in neighboring villages. Musical instruments were provided for bhajan mandlies under social education programme and some sets had been received. A function was organized in the primary school building Debayal. All the members of the mandlies, folk song singers and village youth were invited. Members of my staff were already there. It was a good gathering. Many singers came from villages. Diwan Singh our store keeper and some teachers were good at playing harmonium and sang local folk songs. M. D. Joshi, the compounder took an active part. *Bedu pako bara masa* an old folk song recomposed by Mohan Upraety and Brijendra Lal Sah, was on every one's lips. This song has gained countrywide popularity and its tune is one of the marching tunes of army band. It is sung with great fervour by bandmasters in marriage processions and makes every one dance. The song was sung by the whole group and all danced. It was a superb musical night. From that day onwards we collected in the evening and had interesting musical gatherings. This brought cheer to our life.

I found music a great asset in my service career. It helped me immensely in organizing meetings and changing attitudes of people. I learned playing harmonium and it became my life long companion. Tolstoy has called music the dumb prayer of the soul.

I feel great pleasure in writing a few words about M. D. Joshi, my next-door neighbour. I still remember his tall stature and smiling face. The medical officers posted there would seldom stay. They would either go on long leave or get their transfer for want of amenities and loss of their medical practice. Joshi was serving the area for a long time and was in-charge of the dispensary. His kind and sympathetic behavior endeared him to all. He would attend patients unable to walk to the dispensary on a simple call. Old women whom he treated could not pronounce the word compounder and just called him cumpoter. "Kum" in hindi means little or small and they thought that he was just a little doctor. They wished him to be a "sakar" (bigger in their dialect) doctor. They blessed by saying, "Sunny you are cumpoter now; may you become sakar poter soon." He was very popular and did great service.

The selfless service rendered by people like Joshi needs to be honoured and highlighted. Writers and the media write volumes about leaders and high-ranking officers but good workers at the lower level seldom get any applause. Their good work needs exposure to encourage them and inspire others.

A small grant of 20,000 rupees was received for the remaining two months of the financial year. It was sanctioned to the neediest villages for drinking water schemes. The other needy villages were requested to wait for the next financial year, which was close at hand.

I had now good grasp on my work in field and office. I was fortunate to have a sincere, honest and hard working staff. There was no officialdom and all worked as a perfect team. The short term of the financial year was closing with a good start.

5

The Shabby Money Bag

It was the end of March 1955. I had completed two months in Salt block. My office was well established and work in the field was progressing. Most of the articles ordered for had reached. The grants received had to be utilized before 31st March, the end of the financial year. I, along with Joshi, the accountant, went to Almora to draw money and clear the bills and pay off the staff. I was free from my work on 31st evening. Joshi. had still some work left to do.

"What is your programme Joshi?" I asked.

"I have to be here till the second to collect the bank drafts" Joshi replied.

"Well, I have to settle some transport problems at Ramnagar. Since I have no work here I should proceed to Ramnagar tomorrow. I will leave Ramnagar by bus on 3rd. The bus will reach Mohan by two in the afternoon. Make it a point to reach there in time so that we can go to the block head quarter together".

"I will be there in time", Joshi confirmed.

I reached Mohan by Ramnagar-Sankar bus at two in the afternoon,. Joshi had already arrived and joined me. We reached Sankar at 3. 30 in the evening. Chandra Lal Sah, Assistant Development Officer met me there. As we were preparing for our march, Joshi suddenly said that he had left his bag containing cash, some books etc somewhere and he ran to catch the bus, which was ready to leave for Ramnagar. He gave me no time to inquire how and where he left it and caught the moving bus. It was an unexpected shock. How could he have been so negligent and irresponsible? He left me on the lurch. I could not decide what to do. It was no use staying. Disheartened and worried, Sah and I left for the block headquarters.

It was a restless night. The amount included the pay for the staff and bank drafts for various firms. "What would happen if all these are lost?" It will be a very difficult and embarrassing position for me at the very start of my service. I was already disturbed with my posting in this remote place and this was a new calamity. Whatever courage I had gathered so far slipped away. All these thoughts kept me awake. I got up completely tired the next morning. In no mood to sit and work in the office I visited a neighboring village. Two days passed, and there was no news of Joshi. I got impatient and decided to leave for Almora. Sah requested me to wait for a day more. Weary and tense I went to my room to rest in the evening. It grew dark and as I was lighting the lamp there was a knock at the door.

"Who is there?" I enquired.

"I am Joshi, sir", a feeble voice replied.

I was excited and came out with the lantern.

Joshi wished me. He looked fatigued.

"Sit down Joshi".

"I am too tired sir". He looked pale and downcast as he took the chair.

"I need a cup of tea if I may", he said feebly.

The other members including Sah gathered around.

"Could you get the bag?" Sah asked.

"My throat is dry, let me have tea to enable me to speak".

There was a silence. Joshi sipped his tea, composed himself, looked around and began in a low voice.

"After leaving Sankar that evening Sir, I went to Tarikhet where I had stayed the previous night with accountant of that block. We had worked together in the past."

"How is it that you are here again?" he asked surprised and requested me to take my seat.

"I have come in search of my bag which I have lost somewhere. I was here last night and I thought I may have left it behind".

"You have left no bag here my friend". He brushed aside my assumption.

"Don't play with me my dear, it contained all the money. I will be nowhere if I do not get it".

"Believe me my friend, had it been here I would have been the first man to deliver it to you. You may have left it elsewhere. For your satisfaction you can search my room". He looked at me with a grim face.

"I have no suspicion. Just think the state of my mind, I am in great despair".

"I have all sympathies with you, but what can I do?" He offered me tea and I left for Ranikhet bus station from where I had purchased a ticket for Tarikhet and waited for the bus. I inquired from the booking clerk and other employees who were there but found no clue. My next destination was Almora where I made a thorough search both in the planning office and the treasury but there was no trace of the bag. There was only one place left. On my way back I had gone for a short while to my village near Hawalbagh. "Let me search there", I thought and searched every nook and corner of the house. I was nervous and disillusioned and searched places where I had never been. My father got inquisitive and asked me what I was searching for. I told him it was the bag containing my clothes. I was now broken; there was nothing left and I decided to return to the block and inform about the loss".

"A glass of water please", Joshi was silent again. His lips were dry. Every one of us was looking at him with rapt attention. His tale seemed to be over, I thought and a strange sensation crept into my heart. I tried to gather courage to face the mishap.

Joshi emptied the glass, licked his lips and changed his posture.

"Today", he resumed, "I reached Mohan at one in the afternoon. Physically and mentally exhausted I sat on a bench near the teashop and asked for a cup of tea. Sah the booking clerk of the bus station was sitting as usual in his chair and smoking. There was an hour for the bus to reach. Sah knew me well. He looked at me, snapped his fingers to remove the ash of his cigarette and said, Joshi you were here just the other day and again to day, why these rounds?"

"Nothing special," I said. I wanted to evade his query. I was disgusted and not in the mood to relate my foolish mistakes.

'There must be something Joshi, you look worried and pulled down. Is there any harm in telling me?".

I was moved by his sympathetic tone.

"What shall I tell you Sah", I said. "A great misfortune has struck me."

"What misfortune, may I know?"

"Well Sah that day when I reached Sankar and was ready for the march I found that my bag was not with me. I must have left it somewhere on the way I thought and I ran back to catch the bus to search it out. I went toTarikhet, Ranikhet, Almora and Hawalbagh-, all the places I had been but could not find it".

"What sort of bag? And what was so precious in it that you are so desperate?"

"It had cash, some bank drafts, papers and my clothes. I have lost all that. I do not know how I shall face this calamity".

Sah looked at me closely, stood up and sat near me. He put his hand over my shoulder and said, "Some days back Joshi when I was leaving for my room after my day's work I saw an old, shabby bag lying under the bench. I ignored it thinking some villager may have left it. On second thought I turned back, picked it and took it with me. I live in a forest official's house up on the ridge. I did not think it worth keeping in my room and hung it on a peg in a corner of the veranda, and just forgot about it. The next morning no body came to claim it either. It is three days now and I do not know if it is there. You can't be having such a shabby bag, I am sure."

His words were kindling a ray of hope within me. The description was matching, but who knows if it was still there and that dampened my hope.

"Take me to your house please" I requested him. "Let me see if it is mine and still there".

I stood up in excitement and both of us climbed the ridge. My heart was beating fast and I was in a hurry to reach the top. As I reached near the house and saw my bag on the peg I ran and grabbed it.

Sah, who was watching me, said, "Make sure Joshi it is your bag and see that every thing is intact."

I checked the bag hurriedly and found every thing as I had kept it.

My joy was unbounded. It was a miracle. The bag full of money remained untouched for three days and nights and no body cared to see what was there inside. God had really been very kind.

Sah came close and said, “You have not been fair to goddess of wealth. I would not like to see you with this shabby bag next time”.

‘It has saved me from a great catastrophe. I will preserve it as my savior”.

I thanked Sah for all that he had done for me took the bus for Sanker and I am here.

“But where is the bag?’ I asked.

Joshi stood up went behind the door where he had hidden the bag and kept it on the table. He took out a packet of sweets he had purchased at Sanker and gave it to me.

It was all the grace of God. It is He who helps us in all our ordeals. I distributed the sweets.

All the members of the staff rejoiced. We celebrated the happy ending with some music before retiring for, what would be, a peaceful night’s sleep.

That, however, was not to be the end of Joshi’s tale. After holding staff meeting one April morning I went for lunch. I came back in the afternoon and saw the field staff searching some thing behind the office building. It was windy and drizzling. “What are you searching?” I asked.

“We are searching some bank drafts,” one of them replied. “Joshi was dispatching them to the firms concerned and had spread them on his table. Suddenly a gust of wind came and swept them out of the window. We have found all but one. We have searched every nook and corner.”

I asked Joshi to give me a paper just the size of the bank draft. I took it and stood on the ridge. Wind was still blowing in the same direction. I let the paper fly with the wind. It floated down the valley and dropped a mile away near a mango tree. I asked Prem Lal, the office peon to run to the spot and see if the bank draft is there. We were watching him. He reached the spot, waved his hand and came back beaming, with the bank draft secure in his hand. It was a sequel to the bag episode.

6

A Strange Fish Festival

Manila is a scenic place at a height of about 4500 ft in the Salt Block. There was a high school at Manila, the only one in the block then. A dense pine forest above the village led to a temple of Manila Devi on the hill top. I was touring the area in the month of June and made it a point to spend some peaceful hours in this picturesque place. Next, I planned to tour Talla Salt Patti which falls on the eastern side of the block across Ramganga River. A bridge at Sanker, on the southern edge of the block was the only way across this water obstacle. On the return, Hira Ballav Tiwari, the Village Level Worker of the area was my companion for the trip.

"The river has receded and can be crossed on foot these days", Tiwari told me and suggested to cross it to go to Debail on the other side of the river, instead of taking the long route over the bridge at Sankar.

I agreed and we started early in the morning to avoid the hot sun. It had rained in the night but the morning was clear and pleasant. We passed through the terraced fields, which were being ploughed for paddy plantation.

The road then went down a rugged slope to the river. As we approached the river I saw a big crowd on the other bank.

"Why this crowd?" I inquired.

"They are here to celebrate the fish festival. Villagers celebrate this festival every year during this month all along the river bank. Different dates are fixed for each village. It is the turn of the village on the other bank today", Tiwari said.

We reached the bank of the river, took off our shoes, pulled up the trousers and got ready. Tiwari was tall and well built and offered to take me on his back to spare me the inconvenience! I however wanted to have the experience of going across this large river myself. We entered the river; the water was cool and more than knee deep. The round stones in the riverbed were smooth and slippery and needed a firm stride to avoid a slip. We moved slowly and reached the other end. Tiwari requested me to rest for sometime and added, "the fish festival is about to begin and you must watch it".

The villagers seemed ready with packets of, what I later found, was a paste made of local herbs. They jumped into the river shouting, started mixing the paste in water and stirred it with hands and feet. Moments later, fish started coming to the surface; apparently paralyzed. They were an easy prey and were picked up and passed to the river bank where eager villagers gathered them in big baskets.

It was a hideous mass killing. They were draining the river of all the fish leaving some half dead fingerlings.

The whole place was stinking with the strong odor of fish. I couldn't bear the stench. The villagers were busy in their fish catching spree and enjoying it.

"Let us go", I told Tiwari.

Tiwari told me that they will continue till the last fish is picked and will then distribute the fish among all the families of the village.

A traditional fair, it is celebrated by all villages along the river bank with gusto. The sun was high up in the sky and it was very warm. The climb over the hill was uncomfortable. We reached home late in the evening.

7

A Tearful Parting

It was nearly September end when the monsoon rains finally stopped and the rivulets in the countryside receded and the muddy waters of rivers started turning clear. The air was cool and crisp and touring the villages under a clear blue autumn sky was pleasant. Farmers were busy harvesting millet and chili. Chili is a major crop in the Salt region. The rooftops of the houses shone a bright red with ripe chilies drying on them, adding colour to the countryside.

I was touring the villages, supervising work of drinking water schemes, primary school buildings and attending the meetings of graam sabhas (village councils). The meetings were being held for grassroot formulation of the second five year plan. The villages were faced with multitude of problems. There was scarcity of drinking water, fuel and fodder, lack of irrigation facilities, schools, roads, bridges etc. A phased programme had to be planned. During the long British rule there were no plans for the upliftment of villages. The rulers were concerned with the collection of revenue and maintenance of law and order. The department of agriculture, animal husbandry and cooperation were of course there but they were just showpieces for the world. They had no impact on the farmers who were living in abject poverty, illiteracy and ignorance. They had accepted it as a way of life, a destiny from which there was no escape. It was necessary to arouse in them the longing for of a better life and make them aware of their deplorable condition. Soon after independence a separate department of Community Development was created which was knocking at the doors of the villagers, telling them how, with their personal efforts and help from the government they could improve their living, change the face of the country and lead it to progress. The extension workers were going from door to door explaining the improved methods of cultivation and making available improved veraties of seeds, fruit plants, pesticide etc.

It was now eight months that I was here. My family was finally with me after the birth of a daughter in June. My son and elder daughter were in the village primary school. The members of my staff who had been living with me had found accommodation in the neighboring villages. I had adopted the village life. The urban mentality had taken a rural colour. My mind was now absorbed with the problems of the villages.

My wife was my greatest support all these months. She never complained about my leaving Meerut for this remote part of the country where hardship was a part of life. She encouraged me whenever I was in a depressed mood.

I was sitting in my room one evening. Accountant Joshi came with some of his colleagues. He had returned from Almora that day. He looked sad.

"What is the matter Joshi, you look worried?" I asked.

"There is a very sad news Sir". Joshi said with a gloomy face.

I was taken aback. "What is it?" I asked.

"You have been transferred to Joshimath, a new block that is being opened in Garhwal District. We do not want you to leave us and we will not let you go."There is a ray of hope, he added. "The District Magistrate has requested the government for the cancellation of your transfer".

We talked till it was dark about the days we had spent together.

I was now in a fix. After crossing all the hurdles in early months I had settled down and was engrossed in my work. There was a loving bond with the people and close attachment with the staff with whom I never maintained a distance. We all lived and worked like brothers in a family.

But the other side of the picture was also there. Joshimath was a place close to the famous Himalayan shrine of Lord Badrinath. Was this a call from the wonderland; the abode and playground of Gods? Was it the fulfillment of my dreams of younger days when as a student at Nanital I climbed the Snow View hill to look at the snow peaks and longed to be there? The lure of the Himalayas stirred my heart. How was I to decide?. I left it to providence.

I met Chand the District Planning Officer after a couple of days at his Almora residence.

"You have been transferred" he said, "I have tried my best for cancellation of your transfer but the government does not agree. You have worked hard and established things well in that remote area and I doubt if the tempo will be maintained. I have however requested for the stay of your transfer till the second five-year plan is completed. You have to work on it. I will relieve you after that".

"I was lucky to have you as my boss. It was your guidance and encouragement that helped me."

Chand was one of the most honest and sincere officers I have worked with. Whenever we were on tour together or he visited my block he never allowed me or any other person to spend a single paisa. If ever I tried to open my purse after having tea in some restaurant he would say, "Do you get better pay than me?", and would push my purse in my pocket. He was very good at heart.

I was back at my block.

I systematized the work in the field and office to prepare a model plan. I had already started work at gramsabha level. These plans were now ready. They were scrutinized and were discussed, amended and passed in the block advisory meeting. Laxmi Lal Sah my assistant worked very hard. His compilation and typing of the plan was meticulous. The whole process took two months.

I went to Almora to present the plan to the district planning officer.

"You are the first to submit the plan", he said, "You must have done it in a hurry".

"It is for you to examine it," I said with a smile.

Brij Mohan Pandey Deputy Project Officer was sitting there.

Chand did a cursory reading and turned to Pandey. "Take it, discuss it with other district heads and let me have your comments".

We went and discussed it with the agriculture, animal husbandry and cooperative officers and met Chand in the evening.

"The plan is perfect in all respects", Pandey told Chand. "It is comprehensive and well compiled".

Chand was pleased and gave me the relieving order.

Chand invited me to his residence to talk about the old times spent together and we parted with heavy hearts.

The parting time was close. There was a dismal look on all faces and gloom all around. The staff and local people gave a farewell. Laxman Singh Adhikari, a freedom fighter and social worker came all the way from his village and expressed the love and good wishes on behalf of the people of the block. Chandra Lal Sah representing the staff spoke a few words, became emotional and sat down with a chocked throat. Joshi was in tears I could find no words except tears, which perhaps is the true expression of the heart and makes words superfluous.

Such affiliation and closeness in colleagues seems improbable today. But those were the times when honest people came together and worked for common causes and friends and relationships were valued.

On 12th December1955 I left for Joshimath with my family. Some members of staff accompanied me up to Ramnager and the rest wished me a safe and pleasant journey with tearful eyes at Debail.

On my way I was reminded of the day I had come to join my duties here. The barren hills, which had looked bleak and cheerless then had now a charm, looked homely and intimate as if I knew them since ages. We reached Ramnagar that day at about seven in the evening and stayed there for the night. The bus for Kotdwara, on way to Joshimath, was ready at eight next morning. All members of my staff who had come surrounded me, beheld me with tearful eyes. My wife was also weeping and I was in tears. The sight moved even the passengers and other people at the bus station.

It was the most touching and painful parting in my life. The bus started moving, and with it the most memorable stay of eleven months had come to an end.

Fifty years have passed. The world has changed as never before. We are in an age of super computers, Internet and sophisticated mobile phones. I do not know how that area may be today. I heard that Marchula and Manila were connected by motor road long ago. The fear and fury of Badangad River must be an old grandmother's tale now.

Memory of days spent there is still fresh in my mind. It was here that I learned my first lessons on community living, field and office management. It was here that I learned how to mould and adjust to the abrupt and major changes in life and face problems with courage. Above all I learned how to love and be loved by staff and people and find the image of God in the hearts of the simple, innocent men and women living in distant remote corners of our country. The experience I gained helped me to face greater challenges in life. Whatever success I earned in my service career, I partly owe it to the foundation laid in those eleven months and the love and regard I got from the staff and the people.

I thank my stars for my first posting there.

8

The Joshimath Days

It was the second day of our long journey from Debail to Joshimath. The bus made its way on a fair weather gravel road. The tearful parting at Ramnagar was fresh in my mind even as I watched the countryside slip past. We were now entering the forests of Corbett National Park, then called Hailey National Park. Jim Corbett the famous hunter, who had saved many lives from the man eating tigers in Kumaon persuaded Sir Malcolm Haily, the then governor of U. P. , to convert this area into a national park. The government declared it a sanctuary in 1935 and named it Hailey National Park. It was subsequently renamed Ramganga National Park in 1955 but in 1957 it was rechristened as Corbett National Park in memory of Corbett, the great naturalist, conservationist and lover of wild life specially the tiger, whom he called "the large hearted gentleman". I remember as a student in Nanital, Laxmi Lal Sah a close friend, often talked of Corbett (his elder brother, himself a hunter, was supposedly known to Corbett) and related stories of his hunting man-eaters. I myself never got a chance to see this great man. Corbett has written many books in which he gives very interesting account of his adventures and encounters with the man-eaters.

At the time of its inception the Park had an area of about 158 square km but now it covers an area of 1319 square km. Two thirds of its area falls in Garhwal and the rest in Nanital district. The Park abounds in wild life. There are tigers, leopards, elephants, cheetals, sambhars, kakars, Neel Gai and several other animals, besides different kinds of birds, fish and reptiles. There are several species of trees like Sal, Sheesham, Haldu, Amaltas and Amla. The Park has grasslands, which provide a good habitat for deer and other herbivorous animals.

The rich wild life and excellent location of the Park attracts thousands of visitors each season between September and June.

The bus was passing through the undulating dense forest area. We saw a herd of deer taking cover among trees in the distance.

It was mid December and a pale winter sun was peeping through the thick foliage of the trees. It was a pleasant drive through the forest.

We reached Kotdwara in the afternoon of 13th December 1955 and stayed in the soldier board guesthouse near the railway station. Kotdwara is situated at the base of the Himalayan foot hills. It is a sub montane narrow strip extending from southwest to southeast and makes the southern boundary of Garhwal. The local people call the area Bhabar.

My first visit to this place was in December 1933 when my father retired from service and the whole family shifted to Chami, our village, about 30 miles from Kotdwara up in the hills of Garhwal. I was thirteen years old. Kotdwara was then a small place. There was a teashop in a hut near the railway station and a small market at a distance of about a furlong. It was connected with Najibabad on the main railway line in the year 1897 and by a cart road to Dugadda and Lansdowne in 1909. This cart road was subsequently improved and converted to a motor road.

A few buses took passengers coming by train straight to Dugadda 16km up along the Khoh River. Situated on the right bank of Khoh River, Dugadda was then a very flourishing town and the main market for the whole of Garhwal. It was from here that the bridle roads to Pauri the district headquarters, Srinagar an important town on the pilgrim route, and to all other places on pilgrim route to Kedarnath, Badrinath and places in lower Garhwal started. Food grains and other essential commodities like sugar, jagggery, cloth, oil, soap etc were transported on mules. Hundreds of mules loaded with these commodities would leave for different destinations early in the morning and there would be another hundred returning back in the evening for reloading the next day. The town would stink with the mule dung.

Kotdwara grew into importance after it was connected by motor road with Pauri and other interior towns of Garhwal. It became the wholesale market for Garhwal and Dugadda lost its importance. I was told by my close friend Lt Col B S Rawat that he vividly remembers the day when the first bus belonging to Lala Makhan Lal, a prominent dealer of Kotdwara and driven by Dayal Singh reached Pauri in the after noon of a day in the last week of March 1943. He was in class five then and the boys ran to bus station from their classes on hearing the horn of the bus. There was a great jubilation in the town and people came with garlands to welcome the bus and its passengers, the prominent one being Biseshwar Dutt

Nautial, the Executive Engineer and Ganesh Prasad Chandola the Junior Engineer of P. W. D. Credit for the construction of this important life line of Garhwal from Dugadda to Pipalkoti goes to these two officials, besides several contractors and laborers who worked hard for its construction. The Motor road from Pipalkoti to Joshimath was constructed under the supervision and efforts of K. N. Thapliyal, Executive Engineer Garhwal and L. D. Gairola Assistant Engineer Joshimath and was completed in 1958. The road from Joshimath to Badrinath was constructed by the Border Road Organization.

It was Uma Nand Barthwal who organized and established the Garhwal Motor Owners Union and managed the transport system of Garhwal efficiently during its infancy.

The topography and climate of the hills and valleys varies as you proceed from the foothills towards the snow line. Most Garhwal hills are high, steep and rugged as compared to the Kumaon hills, which are less in height and have undulating features. Nature has given a step motherly treatment to Garhwal. The traveller is struck by the contrast while entering Garhwal from the east or west. After climbing over the Kausani hills of Almora in the east as you cross Gwaldom, you face the rugged scenery of Garhwal hills. While entering from Kotwara on the southwest you face the outer Himalayan range which starts from the Neelkanth hill above Laxmanjhula and extends along Silogi, Langurgarhi, Kalongarhi, Nainidanda to Deepadanda in the East on the border of Almora district. Garhwal thus was shut off from the rest of the country for centuries in the past. This high range stands as a barrier and checks the monsoon winds resulting in heavy rain on the southern side and comparatively scarce rains in the hinterland. There is a second high range, which starts from Byasghat on the left bank of the Ganga in the West and extends along Adwani, Pauri, Khirsu and goes up to Dudatoli in the East. This range serves as a second barrier. Rainfall reduces further in the valleys of Srinagar, Deoprayag and Tehri. These high ranges tend to make the lines of communication tenuous. There is a climb from Dugadda to Gumkhal and a sharp descent to Satpuli and again a steep climb from Jwalpa to Pauri followed by a descent to Srinagar.

We left Kotdwara next morning at eight and reached Dugadda in an hour. From Dugadda there was one-way traffic called the gate system, as the road then was narrow. Timings were fixed for the departure of the vehicles, which would stop at fixed places on the route and wait for the vehicles coming from the other direction.

While waiting at Dugadda I was reminded of the old days when there was no motor road and I along with my younger brother and two cousins would walk a distance of 20 miles to our village when our school at Nainital closed for winter vacations. Each one of us carried a heavy bag full of books, clothes, packets of parched gram and *elayachi dana* (sugar balls) etc on our backs. Walking on the rough foot track as it twisted and turned with the sharp contours of the hills was tiresome but the journey had its thrills as well. Crossing more than knee deep water of the Western Nayar River at Dangal and Eastern Nayar at Baunsal was great fun as was cooking meals at Raitpur, a place mid way. There were no bridges on these rivers and no restaurants as exist today. The shopkeeper would provide you with rations and utensils to cook.

My mother and aunts, happy to see us after a year, would embrace us and distribute the gram and sugar balls to all the families in the village. Every one would know about our arrival. This custom was religiously followed in those days and kept all the families together in a loving bond. Winter was the time for fun and merriment. We had a Ramlila club in the village and there would be plays from the Ramayan and the Mahabharat in which we took active part. The most popular play in those days was "Amar Singh Rathor". Occasionally there would be folk songs and dances followed by a contributory dinner. The married girls would come to their *Maika* (mother's place) during winter months and would sing sweet songs in an open *chabutara* (platform) till late night. These customary community entertainments have vanished now. Migration to the plains is another factor responsible for the decay of community life in the hills.

The policeman gave the signal for the fleet to move with the first vehicle carrying a red flag and the last one a green one. It was a clear day and after negotiating several bends of the mountain slopes, covered with sal forests on the lower reaches, and pine on the higher slopes, we reached the top from where Kalaundanda, a military station was visible. It is called Kalaundanda by the locals probably because of a dense forest at a height of 1800 meters. The Garhwal Rifles moved here in 1887 on the suggestion of D. Campbell the Deputy Commissioner of Garhwal and approval of Brigadier General Murray G. O. C. Ruhelkhand. The town was named Lansdowne after Lord Lansdowne, the then viceroy of India.

Our bus stopped at Gumkhal, a small place about 5000ft high above sea level. From here the first view of the majestic Chaukhamba and its neighboring peaks stirs the heart and one bows to the Abode of the Gods. The road descends down in numerous bends to Satpuli, 56km from Kotdwara, in the valley. Situated on the left bank of the Western Nayar River, Satpuli was a small village. It grew into a prominent town gradually after it being connected by motor road in 1943. It took the authorities a long time to construct a permanent motor bridge over the Eastern Nayar and thus it remained a mid way halt for many years. A temporary wooden bridge used to be constructed after the rains in October which served till June. A pedestrian suspension bridge was put up later and transshipment was done during the rains. A number of buses would be parked on the other side of the river to ply on Pauri side. A terrible tragedy occurred in June 1951 when the river was blocked some miles upstream. The water started gushing out in the night and raised the river level. The buses parked on the right bank were caught in the flash flood. The bus drivers, conductors and some passengers who were sleeping in the buses were caught unawares. They tried to load the vehicles with stones to avoid being washed away but to no avail. All the vehicles together with the occupants were washed away in broad day light in full view of those on the opposite bank. Had the authorities constructed the bridge in time, this grim tragedy would have been avoided. A song has been composed by a local poet in memory of those who lost their lives, which I have often heard people singing in the hills.

Satpuli occupies a central place in lower Garhwal and is now well connected to all the important places like Pauri on the north, Naugaonkhal on the northeast, Pokhara on the east, Kotdwara on the south, and Banghat on the west. It is now a tehsil headquarter. Both the Western and Eastern Nayar meet at a little distance from Satpuli.

From Satpuli there is a level road along the left bank of eastern Nayar up to Jwalpa where stands an old temple of goddess Jwalpa Devi. It is one of the most holy shrines of lower Garhwal. Devotees come to worship the goddess all year round. There is a rush of worshippers during Navratras. Jwalpa has a Sanskrit school managed by a committee. The whole complex has developed into a good religious and educational center due to sincere efforts by the committee members, especially its devoted president D. P. Thapliyal.

A couple of hours drive later the bus reached Pauri. Situated at an altitude of 5,390ft above sea level, Pauri commands the most panoramic view of the long line of Himalayan peaks. In front of you is the great expanse of Alakananda and Mandakini valleys on the Northeast and the Tehri hills on the West with a border of forested mountains. Behind these is the long curtain of snow, a galaxy of peaks, starting from Bunderpoonch(20,731ft) in the extreme west to Trisul(23,490ft) in the far east, with majestic Chaukhamba(20,000ft) glittering like a crown in the center. The setting sun was casting its last rays on the white snow peaks as we entered my younger brother's house for the night's stay.

The British rulers, who defeated the Gurkhas in 1815, added Kumaon and a part of Garhwal (on the eastern bank of Alaknanda), to their territory. Garhwal was declared a new district in 1839. Srinagar which was the capital of the Garhwal kings till 1803 and of Gurkhas from 1803 to 1815 was not liked by the Englishmen because of its warm and unhealthy climate. The cool and bracing climate of the Kandolia hill just above Pauri village at a distance of eight miles from Srinagar attracted them and Pauri was made the headquarters of the new district in 1840. Pauri started developing into a new hill town with the construction of bungalows, a dakbungalow, the Court, and all the paraphernalia which went with the district headquarters of those times. It was connected with all important places in the district by foot tracks. The road from Dugadda, the last motor terminus of Garhwal was especially well maintained. Passing through Dadamandi and then ascending to Dwarikhal it descends to Banghat on the bank of the Nayar River. There is a gradual ascent up to Adwani from where it is a level path through a dense forest to Pauri. There are dakbungalowes at all these places on the 38 mile road from Dugadda.

The Englishmen had a fancy for the hill districts and almost all the Deputy Commissioners during their long rule were Englishmen. They not only maintained the natural beauty of the hills but added by planting trees all along the Adwani-Pauri road. You can still see a row of tall deodar trees along this road and around old residential and office buildings. An old resident of Pauri once told me that there was one Deputy Commissioner who did a lot of plantation. He was leaving Pauri for England on retirement. His personal luggage had already been dispatched to Kotdwara and he was to leave the next day. He received a parcel of seeds he had ordered from England. He postponed his departure, got the seedbeds prepared and sowed the seeds himself. He instructed the gardener about the requirement of irrigation, method of transplantation of the seedlings, future care and the places where the seedlings were to be planted.

The British administrators had a special liking for the hill districts, which were considered a prize posting. Philip Mason, the Deputy Commissioner of Garhwal from 1936 to 1939 calls it his best job in India.

Some English Deputy Commissioners have left beautiful and interesting accounts of their stay, contacts with the people and charming descriptions about their wanderings in the Himalayas. It is through them, their books that we peep into our own hills and the past. Atkinson's Himalayan Gazetteer is still the last word on our hill districts. There is no book on Garhwal, which does not quote Atkinson. It is an encyclopedia, a treasure of valuable record covering all aspects. H. G. Walton's book "Gazetteer of Garhwal Himalaya" is another informative book on the district. P. Mason in his interesting book, "Witch Sweet Witch" and "A Shaft of Sunlight" gives graphic description of the social fabric in remote villages of Garhwal. He loved the people as his friends and says that they have the virtue of simplicity, fidelity, courage and power to endure.

Vernede was another Deputy Commissioner who toured the district extensively. He had special fondness for the inaccessible areas. He built a hut called the Vernede Hut at Bedni Bugiyal (11000ft) and took a great interest in the district. I had a chance to go through his project report on the proposed Marora dam on Nayar River. He says that he has written it as a layman. The project reflects his extensive knowledge about the area and his grasp of a highly technical subject. The U. P. Government shelved the project as the experts said that it was not feasible.

Narayan Singh, a resident of Joshimath told me that Vernede was fond of skiing on the gentle slops of Auli bugiyal (10,000ft above sea level). He would send Vernede a telegram after the first snow fall at Auli who would then walk all the way from Pauri, a distance of 90 miles and take Narayan Singh to Auli for skiing. Incidentally, Auli is now a famous skiing resort.

Pauri could have developed into a good hill station had the authorities paid attention to its planned development and stopped haphazard constructions. It gained more prominence on the creation of a separate Garhwal Division in 1969.

We left for Pipalkoti next morning. A descent from Pauri on the winding road took us past a spur with a commanding view of the wide Alaknanda valley. The snow peaks in the far distance gave a perfect background to this panoramic view. The town of Srinagar lay in its lap close by. Situated on the left bank of the Alaknanda and on the main pilgrim route to Badrinath and Kedarnath, Srinagar has seen many ups and downs in its long history.

Srinagar is named after a natural Sri Yantra (mystical diagram with supernatural powers) on a huge rock in Alaknanda River. It is here, legend says, that Lord Vishnu worshipped Shiva with a thousand lotus flowers at the temple of Kamaleshwer. One flower fell short. Vishnu prepared to offer his eye when Shiva appeared with the flower he had stolen to test Vishnu. Shiva was pleased and gave him the Sudarsan Chakra.

The Adi Guru Shankracharya stayed here for some days during his long journey from Kerala to Badridham and it was here on the bank of the Alaknanda that he perceived the power of goddess Durga and composed his famous hymns in praise of the goddess.

The small town came into prominence in 1500 A. D. when Raja Ajaypal shifted the capital of Garhwal from Dewalgarh to this place. It flourished as a center of art, literature, architecture and music of Garhwal for a long time. Maularam, the famous poet and artist lived here in the court of Garhwal kings in the last half of the eighteenth century. The town including the palace of the maharaja was washed away in the floods caused by the bursting of the Gauna Lake in 1894. There was no loss of life as people were alerted in advance. The new town was rebuilt on a higher ground some distance away from the river with well laid out and wide streets.

The town was again deserted after the defeat of the Gurkhas by the British in 1815. The British occupied the part of the Garhwal kingdom lying on the left bank of the Alaknanda and made the Raja shift to Tehri. Pauri was made the headquarters of the district of British Garhwal in 1840. Srinagar regained its lost glory after the establishment of the Institute of Technology, the Polytechnic and some offices of the Hydel and Irrigation Department. The opening of Garhwal University in 1973 made it the educational centre of Garhwal attracting students from all over. It is now a big town and is spread over both banks of the Alaknanda.

We resumed our journey after breakfast. The bus halted at Rudraprayag, the confluence of the Alaknanda and the Mandakini, at Karanprayag, the meeting place of the Pinder River and the Alaknanda and Nandprayag where the Nandakini meets the Alaknanda. We reached Pipalkoti late in the evening and stayed in the Kalikamli dharamshala at night.

I found myself in a different world the next morning. The place was surrounded by lofty mountains over 10,000ft high on both sides, with huge rocks dotted with pine trees on slopes. Pipalkoti is situated on the left bank of Alaknanda which flows in a deep gorge at a distance and is not visible from here. It is the gateway for Joshimath block as the whole area of the block consisting of Talla Painkhanda and Malla Painkhanda Patties lie behind mountain ranges that flank the Alaknanda and its tributary the Dhauli Ganga beyond Vishnuprayag.

Pipalkoti remained the bus terminus for many years. The pilgrims make arrangement for porters, ponies and palanquins from here. I arranged for mules for my luggage.

It was a clear day and walking on a well maintained bridle path shaded with trees and lofty mountains on both sides had a unique charm, especially after three days of rough journey on a dusty motor road. The pilgrim season had ended in the first week of November and there was little traffic on the road. The warm winter sun peeping through the foliage added to the freshness. The foaming Alaknanda was roaring below in the gorge. We halted for a while near the temple of Garur Bhagwan, (the celestial vehicle of Lord Vishnu). The place is called Garur Ganga. Pakhi is a village just above, with well-terraced fields and a dense forest. Tangri was the next halt where a fair, tall, middle-aged man saluted me and introduced himself as Mohan Singh Rana, Village Level Worker, posted there. "I just learned about you, Sir, from the mule driver who is carrying your luggage", he said. "You did not intimate the date of your arrival; I would have come to Pipalkoti to receive you".

"It was a long journey and I was not sure about the exact day I would reach", I replied.

Rana introduced me to the local people. He reminded me of Hira Ballabh Tiwari of Salt block. "All good men are alike", I thought and took an instant liking for him.

It was a sight to see some villages on the other side of Alaknanda hanging like small cradles, on the steep rugged mountain, with narrow terraces wherever they could be made and ploughed by small bullocks. A narrow path looking like a thread from the distance connected them to a rope bridge down below on the Alaknanda. Rana pointed out a cultivated area surrounded by rocks on all sides called Gauvale and said, "long ago, a cow while grazing on the upper slopes slipped and fell down. The cow was pregnant and gave birth to a calf there only. The owner searched out his cow and with great labour made a path by cutting a little part of the rock. On reaching there he found the place fit for cultivation. There was a spring of water as well. He built a hut and is living there with his family since then".

Helang was the next stop on our foot journey to Joshimath. It is a good halting place and we made ourselves comfortable in the panchyatghar building. N. D. Pandey the Principal of Teacher's Training School at Joshimath was camping there with his trainees. It was a pleasure to meet them. The boys presented a rich cultural programme in the night.

Pandey invited me to the closing ceremony of the camp the next day. I sent my family to Joshimath with some of my staff and stayed back to attend the function. We left for Joshimath in the afternoon. The clouds were gathering and it was snowing on the high mountain tops lending a chill to the already cold mountain air. After a climb up to Jharhkula the road passed through a dense oak forest and crossing the Singhdhar ridge we reached Joshimath in the evening.

The Joshimath block was opened on 2 October 1955. A spacious building belonging to the Badrinath temple committee had already been taken on rent for the office and residence of the Block Development Officer. My wife and children had reached and had settled down by the time I was there.

The house once belonged to late Swami Narvada Nand who had planted a good orchard. The compound was full of apple, apricot, pear, peach and walnut trees. There were beds of roses, dahlias, gladiolus, narcissus and several other flowers which bloomed in summer and autumn. The secretary of temple committee one day told me that a snake lived in the false ceiling of my house. It was supposedly harmless and non poisonous and an old resident of the place! He asked me to tell my staff not to harm or disturb it. This somewhat unwelcome neighbor created fear in us. However the snake lived up to its reputation and did no harm. I saw it only twice warming itself under the sun at a corner of the compound. It proved to be an ideal neighbor!

It was a great relief to reach our destination after a long journey of six days. None of us, however, felt tired. We visited the old temples of Narsingh Bhagwan, Vasudev and the temple of Nav Durga besides taking a round of the market.

Joshimath is situated at an altitude of 6,107ft on the left bank of the Alaknanda some 1500ft above its confluence with the Dhauli Ganga. It is from here that the routes to Badrinath and village Mana along Alaknanda and to Niti along Dhauli River bifurcate.

Joshimath in the fifties was a Gram Sabha but had the amenities of a small town. It had a market, a post and telegraph office with a telephone, a dispensary, police post, a dharamshala, a dak bungalow and a guest house belonging to the Badrinath Temple.

Joshimath has a great historical past. Adi Guru Sankaracharya in his mission to spread and expound the tenets of Vedanta philosophy visited this place sometimes during 7th century A. D. He performed penance in a cave under an old mulberry tree which is still there today. He established a monastery called Jyotirmath just above the cave. There is controversy about the period of Sankra. Madhava-Vidyaranya says that most probably he must have lived somewhere between 5th and 7th century A. D. Joshimath thus must have been a prominent place much before the seventh century.

Joshimath was the capital of the Katyuri kings who ruled over Garhwal and Kumaon between 740 to 1,000 AD. Atkinson says that their kingdom extended from Sutlej in the West to Gandaki on the East and from the snow-clad mountains in the North to Ruhelkhand in the South. Basantdeva, a Katyuri ruler, who was also called Basudeva, built the Basudeva temple. The name of the Katyuri king Sri Basudeva Giriraj Chakra Churamani is inscribed on the temple. There is a black stone statue of Vasudeva (Lord Visnu) in the temple and the statue of Lord Garuda. It is a brass image of a very handsome male with wings, wearing the sacred brahminical thread. It is an extremely attractive statue and some ascribe it to be of Bactrian-Greek workmanship.

The other prominent temples are the Nav Dugra temple and the Nar Singh temple. Nav Durga temple is close to the Basudev temple and has nine idols of Durga pasted with thick coat of butter.

Nar Singh temple is dedicated to Nar Singh bhagwan, an incarnation of Lord Vishnu. One arm of this idol is getting thinner. Legend has it that when the arm falls off, Badrinath shrine will become inaccessible as both Nar and Narayan mountains will give way and close up at Patmela near Vishnuprayag. Lord Badrinath will then be worshipped at Subhain, a place twelve miles to the East of Joshimath towards Niti.

I took charge of my office on 17th December 1955. The office and field staff had already joined. I had to repeat the same exercise as I had done in Salt block. I set my office and then went to Lucknow to place orders for items under different heads. I bought public address equipment. It was a new thing for the villagers. The resounding voice and the music became an attraction and there was a request from the gram-sabhas to play it in their villages.

I toured the block and found great response from the people to undertake development works in their villages. There was a wave of shramdan (voluntary labor) all around. The climate, soil and topography of the block are most suitable for horticulture. There were some apple orchards in Joshimath and citrus fruits like *malta* were grown in the valleys. We started a campaign to expand the area under fruit plantation. The vacant lands around school buildings were also taken up under this scheme. The slogan was "Make Painkhanda the Kashmir of Garhwal".

By the end of January, the development activities were in full swing. It was a pleasure to see the people's participation in all the activities of their villages.

I went to Pauri to attend a meeting in the last week of January. One morning I climbed up to the Deputy

Commissioner's bungalow to pay my respects to Sri Gauri Prasad Bagchi, Deputy Commissioner of Garhwal. Located at a secluded place amidst the dense pine, oak and deodar forest the bungalow is in a beautiful environ. P. Mason, Deputy Commissioner from 1936 to 1939 loved the house. It is a house where he says, panthers roam at night, a house which gives a majestic view of the Himalyan range particularly the massive pillars of Chaukhamba, and above all a house which has a billiard table brought on head load from Dugadda by hundred men long back in 1896.

I met Bagchi at about 9-30 in the morning. There was no other visitor. A fair, tall and stately person, Bagchi asked me about my previous posting and present activities in the block. There was no bureaucratic air about him and I found myself quite at ease. Little did I know then that this meeting would develop into a life long friendship?

9

The Legend of Goddess Parnkhanda

Joshimath block is also named Painkhanda block. The block consists of two patties-Painkhanda Malla and Painkhanda Talla. Painkahda Talla includes whole of Alaknanda valley from Garurganga in the south to Mana in the north, including the Urgam valley on the right bank of Alaknanda. The Dhauli valley from Joshimath to Niti, a distance of 45 miles comes under Painkanda Malla. Geographically Painkhanda is the largest sub-division of the district but it has far less cultivated area and population. In the past it was one patti under the charge of one patwari. There is a saying, *"Kahan niti kahan mana shersingh patwari ne kahan kahan jana"* (where is niti and where is mana! Where will one shershigh patwari go?).

Vidya Dutt Sati of village Paini told me an interesting mythological story behind naming this region Painkhanda. One morning he took me to a temple dedicated to Goddess Parvati on a high, solitary ridge. The temple was surrounded by tall deodar trees. The place animated spiritual vibrations. We worshiped the Goddess and sat on a spur near the temple, overlooking the Alaknanda valley. It was a cold winter morning. The Alaknanda was flowing in a deep gorge down below. At the far end on the West is the beautiful Urgam valley covered with dense forest.

Pointing to the temple Vidya Dutt told me, "This is the place where Goddess Parvati performed great austerity to win Shiva's love".

He related to me the story of her great penance from Purana. Puranas are the sacred books, the perennial streams of wisdom of great saints, seers and sages, flowing down from the immemorial past.

"Shiva" he said, "is the supreme God. He is the transcendental aspect of Brahman. Sati, the primordial supreme power also called Durga, Parvati, and Kali is the immanent aspect of Brahman. According to Vedanta, creation takes place through the association of Brahman known as Ishwara or Mahadev with Maya, the universal power i. e. the Sakti. Shiva, the supreme God married Sati, the incarnation of the universal kali. She took birth as the daughter of Daksha Prajapati, *manasputra* (mind born son) of Brahma.

Once, a great sacrificial ceremony was held in heaven. All the gods, sages and seers attended it. When Daksha Prajapati entered the ceremonial hall, gods and sages except Shiva, rose and saluted him. Daksha was enraged by discourteous behavior of Shiva, his son-in-law and rebuked him.

After long years, Daksha held a prodigious sacrificial ceremony. He invited all gods but Shiva, as he was displeased with him.

Sati saw all the gods and goddesses going to her father's place. She was tempted and requested Shiva to allow her to go to attend the ceremony. Shiva advised her not to go as they were not invited but Sati could not hold herself back. When she reached her fathers place, Daksha completely ignored her and showed great disrespect to Shiva. Sati felt humiliated and ended her life by her yogic power.

Sati, the inseparable consort of Shiva took rebirth as Himanchal's daughter. Her loving father, the king of the Himalaya named her Parvati. Parvati grew up like the waxing moon. Her hair glistening like the feathers of a peacock, and eyes as timid as gazelle's, made her the most charming woman on earth. Born with a burning desire to wed Shiva, she was always lost in his thoughts.

After the tragic loss of his wife Sati, Shiva was a broken heart and resolved never to marry again. He turned into a great ascetic, went to the solitudes of the Himalayan snow peaks and was lost in deep meditation.

Parvati failed to distract Shiva by her exquisite beauty and charms. But she did not lose hope.

With eyes fixed on the temple Vidya Dutt continued, "Parvati left her home and came to this place to perform great austerities to win Shiva. She left taking food, fruits, and roots and sustained herself upon one leaf. After some days she left taking the leaf as well and was called Parnkhanda (abstainer of leaf). This region was named Parnkhanda after this name. The local people changed it to Painkhanda in their dialect and so the name of our village is Painy".

"It is a long story", he added' "but to cut it short, Shiva's heart melted and he agreed to marry Parvati. He went to her father to beg her hand in marriage. Himanchal and his wife Maina were very happy to give their daughter to Shiva".

"They were married", they say, "at Trijuginarayan, a place 25 miles from Kedarnath, the abode of Shiva. Vishnu, the god who preserves and sustains the universe was the priest. He performed the marriage ceremony which was attended by all gods."

It was a unique story told in an unmatched setting. I felt the presence of the Goddess within and imagined the mother sitting under the tall deodar trees, composed and absorbed in deep meditation, with the image of Shiva in her heart, her mind nay in each pore of her body.

Kalidas, the great Sanskrit poet has immortalized this story in his epic "Kumarsambhav". Shankaracharya in one of his finest hymns Saundarya Lahiri (The Ocean of beauty) has given high place to the goddess whom he calls *tripura sundary* (the most beautiful in the three worlds). In his poetic fancy, he has beautifully depicted a complete union of Shiva with his consort Parvati where in she occupies left half and Shiva the right half of the body. The devotees worship the united form as Ardhanarishwara (half goddess and half god).

It was one of the best mornings of my life. The sun had risen high as we with joyous hearts left the sacred temple.

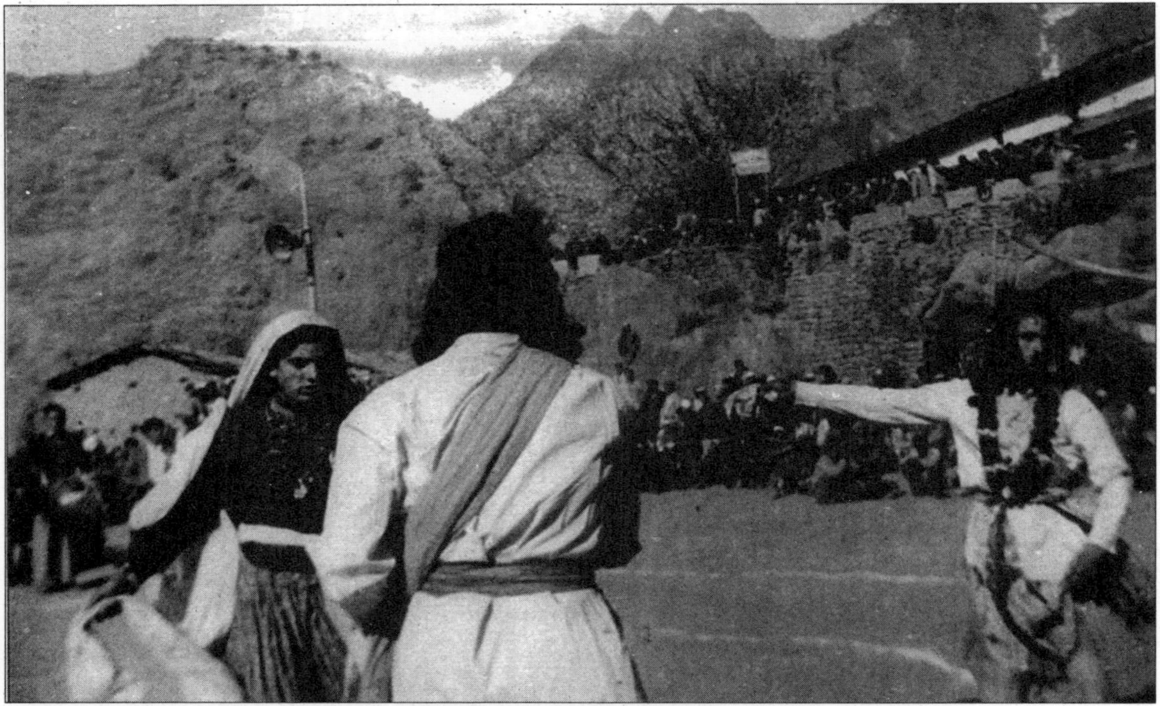

FOLK DANCE AT JOSHIMATH, 1957

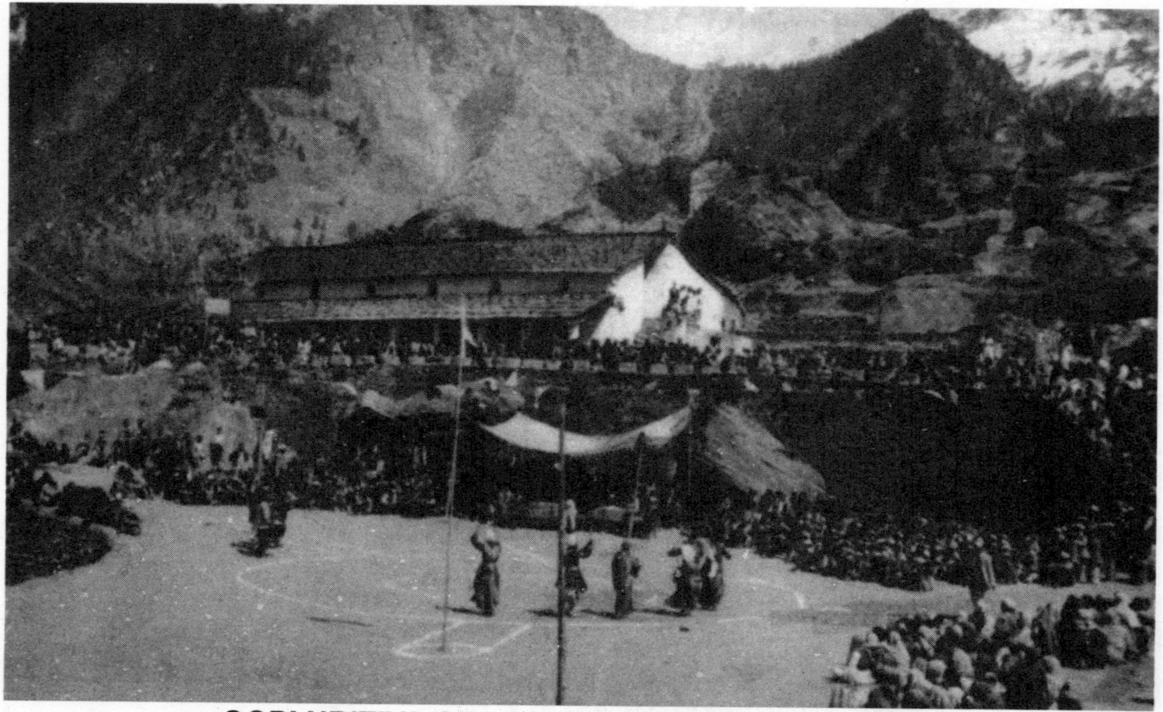

GOPI NRITIYA OF LATA PARTY, JOSHIMATH,1957

10

The Kisan Mela

Melas, *kauthics* and *thaul* as they are commonly called in the hills have been and are an integral part of rural life since immemorial past. Mela means meeting, a get-together on a particular auspicious day of the year. They have a religious, social and spiritual sanctity and provide a platform to the village artists, musicians and folk dancers to perform. They have enriched the varied cultural heritage of the region and made life lively and colorful.

Apart from the traditional ones, a mela was started by Vernede (Deputy Commissioner Garhwal) by incorporating trade and recruitment activities during the Second World War in the spacious ground of Gauchar, a centrally located place on the pilgrim route. He persuaded the Bhotia traders of Niti and Mana valleys to bring their woolen products and the goods imported from Tibet for sale in the mela, resembling the pattern Thal and Bageshwar melas in Almora district. His main object however, was to attract young boys of Garhwal for recruitment in the army. The Second World War was in full swing and the British Government needed soldiers for the army. The Garhwali soldiers had earned fame for their valor in the First World War. Rifle man Gabar Singh and Naik Darban Singh Negi were awarded the Victoria Cross during the First World War. The British had recognized this valor and therefore the added emphasis on recruitment.

The Garhwal Rifles stationed at Lansdown was invited with their band to present colorful performances and this was a great attraction for the youth. The fair caught the imagination of the people and a large number of them flocked to it. The Bhotia traders erected temporary stalls and the Deputy Commissioner and other district officers camped at Gaucher. The whole place turned into a colony of tents. The Gaucher mela is now a permanent feature and is held every year for a week from 14th November.

The impact of melas in the life of the rural people was realized by the community development department. A provision to hold kisan mela once a year was made in the annual budget of the blocks. We decided to hold a kisan mela on the fallow fields of Joshimath in the second week of March. The Village Level Workers gave wide publicity in all the villages one month in advance and invitations with details of programmes were sent to all the gram sabhas and folk dance parties of the block. An exhibition of fruits, vegetables and village crafts was organized. Kripal Singh, the oldest pradhan of the block inaugurated the mela. Villagers came in large number. A big party from Urgam valley came dancing with the accompaniment of drums. There were sports competitions for schoolboys and adults but the most interesting game was the tug of war between gram sabhas. It was great fun, both for the players and the spectators.

A meeting was organized to discuss the problems of farmers and to guide them in improved methods of cultivation, horticulture and breeds of cattle. There were lively discussions and exchange of views. For the villagers it was a new forum to solve their problems.

The star attraction of the mela was the folk dance. The show was held in the afternoon. The border villages have a very rich treasure of folk songs and folk dances. They are based on either the valor of some brave heroes of the past or depict the hard life of the hill people. The *Bagdwal* dance of Pandukeshwar party and the *Gopi* dance of Lata group won the biggest applause from the audience. Nights were packed with cultural programmes and dramas put up by the youth of Joshimath.

It ended with a colorful function of prize distribution and the villagers parted with sweet memories of the mela.

The Janti Fair of Pandukeshwar

In the winter of 1956 the headman of Pandukeshwar panchayat invited me to the Janti Mela.

Janti is an iron tripod put on an open fire to place utensils and cook food. It is widely used in the hills.

The villagers collect in a spacious room near the temple in the evening. A large sized iron Janti is put on the burning logs. The fire continues burning the whole night. People sit at a distance away from the fire and sing traditional songs. At about four in the morning two men who had been worshiping near the fire go to bathe in the cold freezing water of the Alaknanda and come half naked with pitchers full of holy water. The red-hot janti is taken out of the burning fire and exposed on the burning coal. These two men take a round of the fire and one of them lifts the sparking red-hot janti with both of his hands, holds it high up and drops it down on the fire. The bells ring, drums are beaten and men and women sing religious songs. The mela ends with the worship of the village deity and the fire god.

I examined the palms of devotees who performed this miraculous feat and did not find any burn marks. There is no explanation and I presume it a divine power, a miracle.

11

Pilgrimage to Badrinath

Spring is late in the interiors of the Himalayan region. By April the countryside begins stirring with a new life. Snow starts melting on the lower heights. The deciduous trees, which had shed their leaves in autumn, start sprouting new buds, leaves and flowers. The peach, pear, apricot, cherry and apple trees are in full bloom. The oak forests with their new smooth, white and purple leaves look gorgeous. Swift silver waves run through the whole forests as the gusts of the spring winds unfold their leaves. The rhododendrons attract the eye with their red and pink flowers peeping through the green boughs. The roses bloom. Joshimath is well known for its big red roses. The birds that migrate to warmer valleys start returning to their summer habitats.

Preparations for the Badri Kedar yatra start in the second week of April. Pipalkoti was the motor terminus in those days. The bridle road up to Badrinath was repaired. Special labour force was employed beyond Lambaggar where the road gets obstructed with huge piles of snow, mud and boulders that slip down the steep mountains. The medical and health department erected temporary urinals near all the halting places on the route and maintained cleanliness.

After joining in December, I was anxiously waiting for summers to visit the holy shrine of Badrinath, the Valley of Flowers, Hemkund Lokpal and the Niti valley, which are covered with snow during winters. Time to visit these places was just at hand.

The Badrinath temple opens on an auspicious date announced by the Raj Purohit (royal priest) of the Maharaja of Tehri. The date usually falls in the first week of May. Some religious rituals are performed at Joshimath, the winter headquarters of the Rawal, two days before the pilgrimage begins.

Parties of pilgrims from different parts of the country start reaching Joshimath. Every one is keen to reach Badrinath before the temple opens to witness the Akhand Jyoti (eternal flame), the lamp that is believed to be burning since the temple was established.

The Pilgramage Starts

The dictionary meaning of the word pilgrim is a person who goes on a journey to a sacred or holy place as an act of religious devotion. In earlier days people went on *teerth yatra* (pilgrimage) usually in old age after fulfilling their family and social obligations. It was considered a religious duty and a means of seeking salvation. The pilgrimage to the Himalayan shrines was very tough and risky and people went with a conviction that if they met an accidental death they would get liberation.

Pilgrimage in those days had its own charm. You met people from parts of the country you had not seen, listened to unheard dialects and saw men dressed in different kind of apparel. People of all shades, and walks of life moved together with a single mission-a darshan of Badri Vishal.

You saw pilgrims greeting each other and the air resounding with cheers of Jai Badri Vishal, giving divine joy and energy to the body and mind. Pilgrims walking with the help of a bamboo stick, politely asking, "Where are you from baba, mataji, brother, sister? Prompt is the reply, "from Rajasthan, Gujrat, Maharashtra, Kerala, Madras, Bengal, Nepal, Bihar etc" You see a. Stream of people from the East, West, North and South moving to the holy confluence. A perfect unity in diversity.

The pilgrims normally walked ten to twelve miles a day and sought shelter for the night in some dharamshala or a chatti where they got provisions, fuel, accommodation and utensils to cook their meals according to their taste and requirement.

With the advent of the motor road up to the holy shrine the concept of pilgrimage has changed. Tourists outnumber the pilgrims. The journey which was an act of devotion is now a pleasure trip for most of the visitors. The cheer of Jai Badri Vishal is no more heard on the route. The chatties have since been closed and the locals have lost their traditional means of livelihood or turned to lesser alternatives. The dharamshalas are uncared for and several big hotels have come up to cater for the rich.

The pilgrim procession started from Mathagan, an open courtyard near Nar Singh temple at Joshimath. It was headed by the drummers followed by the Gaddi (seat)of Sankaracharya; the Rawal (head priest) was next in a palanquin. A number of pilgrims, who had arrived the previous day so as to reach Badrinath on the opening day and have a darshan of the akhand jyoti "the eternal flame", accompanied the procession which marched with a loud cheer of Jai Badri Vishal (glory to Lord Badrinath).

From Joshimath road descends down to Vishnuprayag. Situated at the confluence of Vishnuganga, roaring down from Satopanth glacier and resounding Dhauliganga from Niti valley, Vishnuprayag is a small place at the foot of a huge rugged rocky mountain standing perpendicular on the bank of the Dhauliganga. The spectacle at the confluence is simply exciting. You see both the rivers come dashing, cascading down the narrow gorges. The rapid current of the voluminous Dhauli pushes the water of the Vishnuganga and keeps its identity up to some distance when they finally unite and form the Alaknanda.

Vishnuprayag is one of the five Prayags, the others being Nandprayag, Karnprayag, Rudraprayag and Deoprayag. Thomas Hardwick, an Englishman who visited this place in 1796 describes it as a town consisting of 800 houses. It appears the town was heavily damaged by the severe earthquake of 1803 and washed away by the subsequent floods, leaving just a narrow strip. Steps have been cut in the rock leading to the Vishnukund at the confluence but it is very risky to take a bath there due to the rapid flow. People just sprinkle water on their body. There is a temple dedicated to Vishnu.

Passing through this gorge with perpendicular rocks I wondered how hazardous the journey might have been when Sankaracharya visited Badrinath in the 7th century. The Gurkhas during their rule from 1803 to 1815 are said to have repaired the road and some bridges. It was Traill, the second Commissioner of Kumaon under British rule who took up the work of constructing the pilgrim route from Rishikesh to Kedarnath and Badrinath in 1827. P. Barron an English tourist wrote in 1842 that the Tories in England criticized Traill for encouraging pagan idolatry.

We passed through Govindghat where there is a big gurudwara with suitable accommodation for the pilgrims. A bridle road bifurcates from here to the Valley of Flowers and Hemkundlokpal across the Vishnuganga. Evening brought us to Pandukeshwar. It is an ancient town on the right bank of the Vishnuganga at a distance of nine miles from Joshimath, mid way to Badrinath. It is named after Pandu, the father of Pandavas who performed penance here. The Pandavas stayed here for some time during their last journey to Swargarohini. There is a temple of Yogbadri one of the five Badries. Some copper plates containing the inscriptions dating to the days of the Katyuri kings are kept here. The other temples are those of Vasudev and Ghantakaran.

The inhabitants of Pandukeshwar consider themselves the descendents of Kuber, the treasurer of the gods. They occupy a prominent place in the management of the Badrinath temple and shift to Bamni Village close to Badrinath, when the temple opens.

The Youth Club of Pandukeshwar was then the most active and progressive one. They took part in cultural competitions and folk dances organized by the block. The gramsabha constructed a panchayatghar at a central place with the assistance of the block and was the hub of cultural activities. I often stayed and witnessed their interesting programmes. Pratap Singh Mehta, a young businessman and press reporter was an active member and gave me detailed information about the Valley of Flowers, Lokpal, and Smythe's conquest of the Kamet peak.

We left for Badrinath next morning and reached Hanuman Chatti. There is a temple of Hanuman on the roadside. It is said that the Pandavas performed a great yagya, (religious sacrifice) here. Half burnt barley grains, supposedly left over from the yagya are still found in some adjoining fields. From Hanuman Chatti the tough climb called the Rarang climb starts. You see Vishnuganga flowing beneath thick layers of snow to a great distance. The road is also covered with snow at many places till June end. The journey was tiresome but the pilgrims who had never seen snow enjoyed and played with it.

After a climb of 3 miles we reached Devdarshani. The very name speaks of a place from where the first celestial view of the divine shrine can be seen. A wide panorama with snow peaks of Nar and Narayan mountains on right and left banks of Vishnuganga suddenly come to view. You bow with a sense of absolute reverence. The sight is thrilling. You have reached the valley of Gods; the abode of Badrinarayan. All your fatigue is gone; you feel fresh and young and there is a cheer of "Jai Badri Vishal" from every mouth. We rested for some time watching the valley with eyes fixed on the holy shrine. It was an easy walk up to the temple.

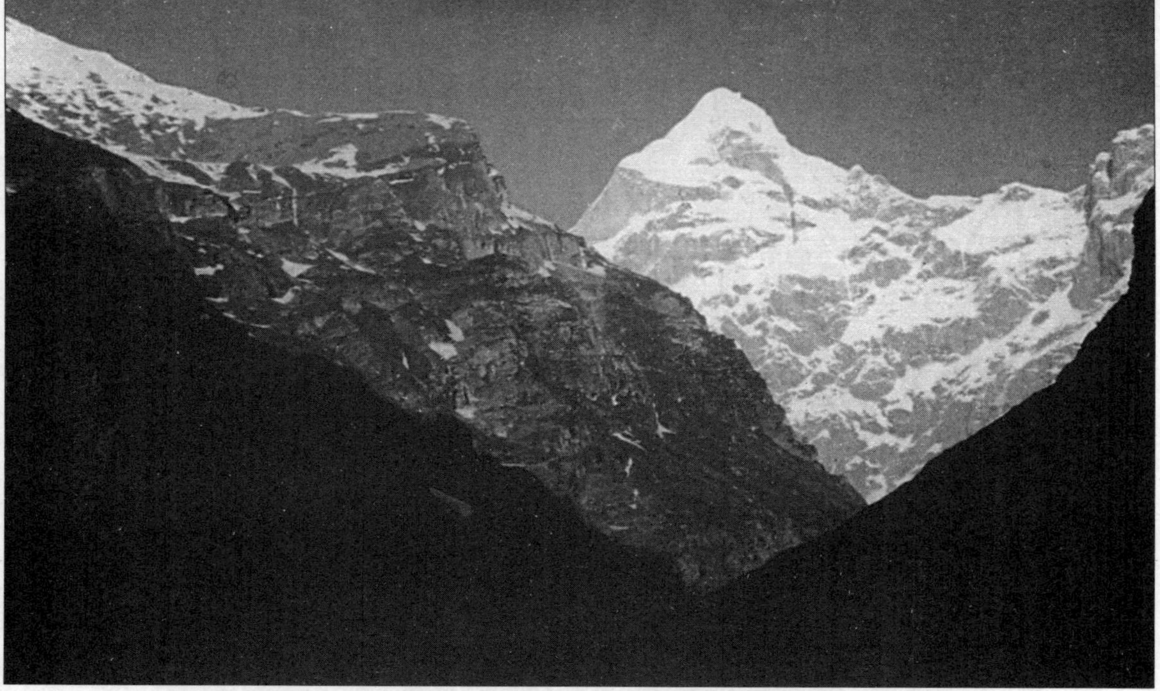

NILKANTH PEAK AS SEEN FROM BADRINATH

12

Badrinath Dham

"The glories of the Himalayas cannot be described in a hundred divine years of Gods. A single glance of the Himalayas can dry up all the sins of mankind."

(Skanda Puran)

In his epic "Kumarsambhava" Kalidas the great Sanskrit poet has called the Himalayas The Divine Soul of God. Each hill, river, peak and valley has been dedicated to some god or sage. It is the perennial source of holy rivers, home for a thousand species of birds and haunt of wild animals .There are temples which vibrate with a divine spirit. Interesting symbolic tales have been woven around many gods, goddesses and sages in the Puranas and the Mahabharata.

The Uttaranchal Himalayas have the privilege of having four Dhams (places of worship). They are Yamnotri, Gangotri, Kedarnath and Badrinath. Pilgrims visiting all the four Dhams complete and conclude their pilgrimage at Badrinath, the most celebrated Dham.

The holy shrine of Badrinath is situated at the foot of the Gandhmadan peak on the right bank of the Vishnuganga, at an altitude of 3110 m. The shrine is 330 km from Kotdwara and 298 km from Rishikesh. Surrounded by the glittering snow peaks of Neelkanth, Narayan and Nar, the temple is in the middle of a three mile long and one mile wide picturesque valley.

Our scriptures say that this Dham was the only place that remained safe from the great floods or the deluge. Manu, the progenitor of the human race tied his boat to a tree and saved himself and his clan. Satpath Brahman (a holy scripture) names the place as Manorawsarpan which is the present Mana village near Badrinath. The Holy Bible also mentions of the great flood and of Noah who took refuge in his boat with seven members of his family.

Jai Shankar Prasad, the great Hindi poet begins his long epic poem "Kamayani" with Manu sitting here under the cool shade of huge rocks of the high Himalayan peak watching the swift flow of the great flood with his wet eyes.

Badrinath has been mentioned in the Vedas, the Puranas and the Mahabharata.

It is said that Shiva and Parvati lived here in a temple near the Taptkund (hot water pool). Once Vishnu came here and was charmed with the exquisite beauty of the valley. He wanted to make it his abode, but dislodging Shiva, the most powerful god, was not possible. He hit upon a plan. He became a child and started weeping. Parvati took pity and wanted to take the child with her. Shiva, the all knower, knew Vishnu's trick and advised Parvati not to fall prey to the illusion. Parvati insisted, persuaded Shiva and took the child to her room. She fed the child and made it sleep on her bed. After some time they both went out for a walk. On their return they found the door bolted from inside. They knocked at the door but Vishnu did not respond. Shiva, the magnanimous god left the place for Vishnu and settled at Kedarnath with Parvati.

It is an interesting story of the two Dhams, one the Vishnu Dham and the other of the Shiva Dham.

Badrikashram or Badrikaranya (Badri forest} has been the tapobhumi (place of penance) of Nar and Narayan, the two sons of the mother goddess Mata Murti. A temple dedicated to her lies about a mile towards Mana village. A fair is held here in October and the Rawal comes to worship the mother. The silver idol of Udhava is brought in a doli to meet the mother. The function ends with dance and music and the idol of Udhava is taken back to the main temple. Ram, Krishna, Indra, Narad, Kuber, Garur and several other gods performed penance here. Sages Vyas, Sringi, Vashist, Muchkund, Markandey meditated here and got liberation.

The great epic Mahabharata was composed and written at this very place. The Mahabharata begins with an interesting story of how the great epic was written in the ancient past. Vyas came to Badrinath and sat in meditation in a cave. All the 100,126 verses of Mahabharata containing the quintessence of the four Vedas, Upvedas, Upnishads, Puranas, history and other sciences were revealed to him. It was a veritable treasure of knowledge. However a problem arose for the great rishi. Who would undertake the stupendous task of writing the voluminous epic for posterity? Lord Brahma appeared before him, and praised him for composing the great epic. He advised him to seek the help of the prodigious Lord Ganesh for the task in mind.

Vyas invoked Ganesh and requested him to write the epic. Ganesh agreed but only on the condition that the dictation by the sage would be without any breaks. The great sage apparently knew the complexity of the task and displaying remarkable foresight, put a condition that Ganesh would write verses only after understanding them. Both agreed and the great exercise began. Each sat in adjacent caves called Vyas Gupha and Ganesh Gupha.

Vyas had composed 8800 very difficult verses and whenever he wanted time for rest or to compose new verses he would recite the difficult ones. Ganesh would take time to understand them. In the mean time, Vyas would be ready with his next verse. It was thus that the great epic of 100,126 verses was completed and preserved as a precious heritage for mankind.

The seven rivers finding mention in the Vedas originated in the Central Himalayas around this dham. The Saraswati River, the most prominent among them originates from Mana peak and meets the Vishnuganga at Kesavprayag near Mana village. Kuber's Alkapuri and his Nandan ban are also in the vicinity of Sumeru peak.

We reached Badrinath in the evening and stayed in the Nepali dharmshala. All the pilgrims were impatient for the temple to open. We got up early next morning and bathed in the hot waters of theTaptkund and reached the temple. There was palpable anticipation in the air as the sealed locks of the temple opened after a ceremony and the Rawal entered the temple with the other priests and the officials. The Akhand Jyoti was brought out for the darshan of all the pilgrims.

The temple is divided into three parts: The Singh Dwar (main gate), the Sabha Mandap (the central hall), and the Garbha Griha (the Sanctum Sanctorum).

The main gate is brightly coloured and exquisitely carved showing Rajasthani style of architecture. It leads on to the Sabha Mandap. In between the main gate and the Sanctum Sanctorum, is the central hall part of which is kept for the devotees who pay for special worship. The rest is for the long queue of pilgrims who enter from the main gate, pass through a railing and move out from the exit gate. On the right side of the hall the Dharmadhikari and some Vedpathis sit on a platform and recite verses from Vishnushahastranam and other holy scriptures.

Sanctum Sanctorum is a small room, 13ft' long and 7'10" wide. The idols of Lord Badrinath and other gods, collectively called Sree Badrish Panchayatan, are placed here. The Badrish Panchayatan consists of Shree Badrinath, Goddess Laxmi his consort, Narayan, Nar, Ganesh, Kuber, Uddhava, Garud and Narad.

Only the Rawal can enter the Sanctum Sanctorum and touch the idols. There is an adjacent room for another priest who keeps articles needed by the Rawal for the worship.

The idol of Lord Badrinath is of black stone 3'9" high. Buddhists who dominated this part of the country in the 6th century and did not believe in idol worship threw the idol in the Narad Kund. Some say the priests had hidden it for fear of its being stolen or damaged by dacoits and as time passed they forgot the place where they had hidden it. Shankaracharya who came here in seventh century salvaged it from the Narad Kund and installed it properly in the temple. He appointed a Nambudri Brahmin from Kerala as the high priest (called Rawal) to perform the worship of Lord Badrinath. He thus established a perennial bond between North and South India.

The Abhishek Puja

The Rawal enters the temple each morning after bath in his private hot water tank near the Taptkund and starts worship of the deity. He gives the idol a bath with cow's milk, curd, honey, butter and holy water brought from the Vishnuganga. The idol is smeared with sandal paste and perfumes, clothed with rich garments and adorned with gold and diamond ornaments. It is garlanded with garlands of fresh flowers and tulsi leaves. The central hall resounds with recitation of verses from Holy Scriptures by the vedpathies. The whole temple reverberates with these holy chants and adds fervor to the already pious mood of the pilgrims.

The long stream of pilgrims waiting at the gate since early hours of the morning starts moving inside the temple as the gate opens. They look at the deity, bow in reverence, make their offerings and move out from the exit door. The guards controlling the crowd do not allow them to stay more then two to three minutes.

I remember a very touching incident on my second visit to the temple in September the same year. Ram Sahay, the Commissioner of the division visited Badrinath along with G.P. Bagchi, the Deputy Commissioner. Ram Sahay offered Abhishek Pooja (a special worship). We were sitting in the front row of the Sabha Mandap. The Rawal was performing the worship of the Lord and the vedpathis were reciting the verses. There was a rush of pilgrims from the main gate and the temple guards were pushing the pilgrims to move forward to make room for others in the queue. A middle-aged lady entered the temple and stood motionless with folded hands. She was completely absorbed in her prayer to Narayan and oblivious to the guards who, none too gently, asked her to move. The

Commissioner happened to see the commotion and the plight of the poor devotee.

"Don't push the lady", he frowned at the guard. "She deserves to sit here not me. Here I am, sitting for over half an hour, just scanning the idol and look at this devout woman. She has not even seen the idol clearly from that distance but seems to have found her Narayan in it. Let her come and sit here".

The woman was conducted to the front row. She prostrated before the Lord and sat with a beaming face full of divine joy and tears in her eyes. The scene left a deep impression in my mind and I still remember it. Only pilgrims like her can feel the presence of Narayan in the deep recesses of their heart. Traveling long distances and bearing hardships they come with a conviction, an unwavering faith that Badrinath is the eternal abode of the Lord. They lose their identity and ego with the blessings of Badri Vishal.

While returning to our rooms the Commissioner told me that he liked the recitation of the verses and would like the vedpathi to write them with translation in Hindi. Mr. Bagchi who was himself a great scholar, volunteered for this task. I gave the verses with the Hindi translation to the Commissioner and told him that it was Bagchi the great Sanskrit scholar who had written the verses. Ram Sahay went to Bagchi and said that he would be his guru thereafter.

Neel Kanth

God has bejewelled Badrinath with a magnificent snow peak called Neel Kanth, "The queen of the Himaliyas" It stands majestically, 21,640 feet above sea level. It is well proportioned with a graceful ice cap that glitters in the sun.

The mountain is associated with Lord Shiva who drank the deadliest poison, Kalkoot and retained it in his throat to save the universe. Viewed from Nar Parvat on the opposite side of the temple, it is an awe inspiring sight.

Mana and Vasudhara

The next day we went to Mana and Vasudhara. Mana is the last border village two miles from Badrinath. It was the place where Manu took refuge during the great deluge.

Situated at an elevation of 10560 ft above sea level Mana is inhabited by Marchas who live in some villages of Niti valley as well. They grow potatoes and millets in fields around the village. Their main occupation was trade with Tibet, which stopped after the war with China in 1962. The people in general were not as prosperous as those in Niti valley but there were some wealthy traders. It is said that one of them lent two lakh ruppees to the Raja of Garhwal to fight the Gurkhas. In winter these villagers migrate to village Ghingran near Gopeshwer.

The Mana people are good craftsmen and make fine woolen carpets and other woolen goods. The women folk are skilled weavers of carpets, socks, stockings and sweaters. During the pilgrim season they do good business as most of the pilgrims visit their village. They display their goods in front of their houses on the wayside for the customers.

In olden days they protected Badrinath valley from the nomadic Tibetan robbers. There is a room in the village where they have kept old weapons which they snatched from the robbers in their fights.

They enjoy certain rights in Badrinath temple. The virgin maidens of the village weave a five yards long and nine inches broad blanket in a single day. The blanket is smeared with butter churned out of the *chawar* cow's milk. This blanket called ghrit kambal (butter blanket) is offered to Badrinath temple. On the closing day in November the Rawal wraps the idol of the Lord in this blanket. The maidens are given gifts for their offering.

The Saraswati River

On way to Vasudhara we passed through the Vyasa cave and the Ganesh cave where the great epic Mahabharata was written. Mana is on the left bank of the holy river Saraswati that originates from glaciers along Mana pass. Fed by the large glaciers north of Mana peak and the long Arwa glacier, the Saraswati flows speedily and disappears into the rocky crevasses before making a dramatic appearance near Bhim Pul. The valley resounds with a roaring sound as its gurgling waters rush out from a huge orifice in the mountain side. The Saraswati holds a very respectable place in Rig Veda. Its bank has been the cradle of Vedic civilization. According to Maxmuller, the German philosopher, it enjoyed greater respect in Vedic age than Ganga in post Vedic period. Descending from a higher elevation than other rivers of the region Saraswati is regarded superior to all the rivers.

The great rishis, Nar and Narayan had their hamlets near its bank and performed penance. Vyasa codified thousands of Vedic verses into Rig Veda, Yajur-veda, Sam Veda and Atharava Veda and taught them to his disciples here.

Just a few yards above the road on the left bank there is a perennial spring of cool, fresh and sweet water said to originate from Mansarover Lake.

Nearby, the Saraswti River flows under a bridge formed by a huge natural rock. It is given the name "Bhim Pul". Legend has it that when the Pandavas were on their last journey to heaven, Draupadi could not cross the foaming Saraswati. The mighty Bhim picked up this rock and fitted it so well that it served as a bridge.

Vasudhara

Vasudhara is three km from Mana. It is a perennial waterfall that drops from a height of 122 meters down the straight barren rocks and is named after the eight Basus (sages) who performed penance here. The sprays that reach the ground are constantly buffeted by winds and it is a common belief that the righteous men get the sprinkling showers while others emerge dry from under it.

Vasudhara is surrounded by dazzling snow peaks of Narayan, Renukutta and Kuber mountains. The solitude, serenity and grandeur of the Himalayas and the songs of the bubbling streams, waterfalls and the sparkling rivers attracted the sages and sanyasies in ancient times to come here for meditation and perform penance.

I had been visiting the holy shrine of Badrinath since 1956. My last visit was in the year 2003. What a contrast! Man's propensity to destroy the environment is in full view. Till the year 1958, habitation was limited to the Narayan Parvat on the right bank of the Vishnuganga and there was no construction on the left bank, except a PWD dak bungalow and a private house of Seth Shanker Dutt Bahuguna. A full fledged town has come up on this side now, with big hotels, dharamshalas, markets, restaurants and other government and private buildings. Opening of the motor road has brought this tremendous change. It has now become an easy trip and draws lakhs of people, young and old, making it a crowded and suffocating place. The celestial serenity has been replaced with a concrete jungle.

I remember when Sampurna Nand, the then chief minister of UP visited Badrinath in 1958 the residents gave him a memorandum in a public meeting and demanded the extension of the motor road from Joshimath to Badrinath. Sampurna Nand said that he was not in favor of Badrinath being connected by motor road. "Let Joshimath remain the motor terminus". He added, "That will save Badrinath from over crowding and also give the pilgrims a real taste of the pilgrimage to a Himalayan shrine". How true it appears now! The modern amenities have undeniably given great comfort to the pilgrim and placed this abode of the Gods within every traveller's reach- which in this age of instant gratification are a must. However the cost of such development threatens the very sanctity of the holy place by wilful destruction of the environment.

Gone are the days when, climbing from Hanuman Chatti, the first glimpse of the holy shrine would stir your heart with spiritual joy and you would feel elated. Instead, now you feel a sense of nausea while getting down at the crowded bus station after an equally nauseating road journey over numerous bends of a rough mountainous road.

The vehicular traffic is increasing every year. While returning back from Badrinath in 2003 I was standing on a ridge and seeing the seemingly endless stream of vehicles moving up. I failed to count the number. The traffic will increase manifold in coming years as the road is being further widened. The ever rising pollution levels are bound to have a disastrous effect on this fragile eco system.

It was once called Badrivan or Badrikaranya (Badri Forest). This proves that there must have been a dense forest in the area, which may have been cut down by the influx of people. Let us make efforts to restore it to its pristine glory and not create conditions to turn the Himalayas into a cold desert.

There have been suggestions from politicians to keep the shrine open even in winter. It is an ancient faith that the gods come here in winter to worship the Lord. This age long belief is symbolic and stands on very strong ground. Let it remain a place for gods, for the divine, during the winters, when it is covered with layers of several feet of snow and not make it a haunt for the tourists. Do not try to put the holy place on a commercial web site1

Swami Tapovan Maharaj who lived from 1886 to 1957 and had his ashram at Gangotri visited Badrinath many times. I close the chapter with his profound words. "Holy land of Badri, May you maintain your glory of nature and glory of spirit till the end of the universe."

Jai Badri Vishal!

13

The Kedarnath Dham

Kedarnath is the Shiva Dham, the abode of Lord Shiva. Shiva is called by a thousand names. He is Maheshwara, Mahadev, the God of the gods, the supreme Lord. He is ever gracious, unborn, changeless, stainless, easily appeased, Lord of the poor and loving master of all the yogis.

Shiva temples exist all over India but the majestic and enchanting Himalaya is his most favorite abode. It is here that he was married to Sati and after her death to her incarnations Ganga and Parvati the daughters of king Himalaya. There are number of Shiva temples in the Himalayan hills but the Kedarnath temple is the most celebrated temple of the Lord. It is one of the twelve Jyuotirlings of India.

Kedarnath is situated in Nagpur pargana of Rudra-pryag district of Uttaranchal state at an altitude of 11,753 ft above sea level. It is 223 km from Rishikesh, of which 209 km is motor road up to Gaurikund and the rest 14 km a foot path. Porters, mules ponies and dandies are available at Gaurikund which is a nice place with a hot water spring, dharamshala, tourist rest house and a dak bungalow. The climb from Gaurikund is tough but enjoyable with green forests, sparkling streams and waterfalls cascading down the steep rocks. River Mandakini flows down in the valley. From Rambara, a small halting place mid way, is a tough climb of 5km and the rugged steep barren Himalayan surroundings appear.

The pilgrims are enchanted when they cross Garur Chatti 11km from Gaurikund and see the majestic Shiva temple with glittering snow peaks in the background. All the fatigue is gone. You are in the land of Shiva.

The temple is built on a flat ridge below the snow peak of Mahapanth. It is a specimen of magnificent architecture built of huge stones nicely cut and shaped by skilled masons. One wonders how those heavy stones may have been lifted and put on the walls. The temple is built on a rectangular platform. There is an idol of a large bull Nandi facing the temple in the courtyard.

Legend from Purana

The Puranas say that after the end of the great battle of Mahabharat the Pandavas wanted to be absolved of the sin of fratricide for killing their own cousins and guru Dronachayara. They went in search of Shiva to pray and request him to absolve them of their sin. Shiva who was displeased with them fled away to Kedar and hid himself there. The Pandavas wandered over the Himalayas and finally traced him at Kedar. Shiva took the form of a bull and got mixed with the herd. The brave Bhima spotted him and ran towards Shiva who dived into the earth. Bhima caught hold of his tail with the result that the hind part remained there and the face 'mukh' appeared at Pashupatinath in Nepal. Shiva was pleased and pardoned them. The Pandavas built a temple at Kedar and worshipped Lord Shiva there. Shiva is worshipped here in the form of the rock symbolizing the back of the divine Lord.

Another story which has been related under the Badrinath chapter says the magnanimous Shiva who once lived in Badrinath Dham left it for Vishnu who liked to live there and came to Kedar. Vishnu felt obliged and ordained that one should first worship Shiva at Kedarneth and then visit Badrinath.

Like the five Badries there are five Kedars and the remaining parts of Shiva's body are worshipped there. The arms are worshipped at Tungnath, face at Rudranath, belly at Madhmaheshwer and hair at Kalpnath.

The Rawal is the head of the temple and lives at Okhimath. One of his disciples performs rituals at Kedarnath.

The Puja

Puja is performed in the temple both in the morning and evening. In the morning it is Nirman Darshan and the devotees offer water and flowers to the deity. In the evening it is Sringar Darshan when the deity is well decorated with garments and flowers and the devotees offer their worship. Arti is performed at the end.

Adi guru Shankaracharya came here at the close of his life in his mission to spread and expound the tenets of Vedanta. He is said to have left his mortal body here. His Samadhi is located at the back of the temple.

The temple is opened on some auspicious day in the last week of April or first week of May and closed after Diwali for winter.

14

Rudranath

Rudranath is the fourth Kedar among the five Kedars. The temple is 18 km from Gopeshwar the headquarters of Chamoli district and is at a height of 11,000ft above sea level. It is about 16 km from Anusuya Devi temple. I still remember vividly my visit to the holy shrine from Anusuya Devi. It was a clear day of September '1965 when I left with a friend for Rudranath at nine in the morning. It is a very tough climb over a steep mountain. Tired and hungry we halted near some huts of villagers who come with their cattle to the rich pastures during summers and rains. A lady was making bread on an oven. She offered us crisp hot bread with fresh butter. It was a great treat. I was touched with the loving hospitality of the simple hill woman. We resumed the march. Suddenly the sky gathered clouds and it started raining followed by a hail storm. We took shelter in a cave. Soon the sky was clear and we reached the top at five in the evening. The snow peaks of Chaukhamba Neelkanth and Dronagiri were shining in the evening sun.

The alpine meadows of Rudranath are some of the best meadows full of flowers and green grass. In between are large stretches of rhododendron bushes. What a scenic beauty it must be when the bushes might be in full bloom in June, I thought to myself and wished I would be here at that time. We reached the temple just before dark and stayed in the temple dharamshala.

The temple is located in a cave fixed with doors. The face 'mukh' of Shiva called Swayambhu Mukhar bind is worshipped here. It is said that Pandavas came here in search of Shiva who hid himself in a cave. The idol is of black stone and a specimen of perfect craftsmanship.

Some distance down the temple is a spring of fresh water and a pond called vaitarani. There is a remarkable idol of Lord Vishnu lying on the coils of Sheshnag.

The Bhatt Brahmins of Gopeshwar are the priests of Rudranath. The deity is worshipped at Gopeshwar during winters when the temple is closed.

15

Tungnath

The temple of Tungnath is on the highest elevation in the Himalayas. It is at the height of 3680 meters above sea level. The temple is 3 km from Chopta which is a very tough climb. Chopta is 30 km from Okhimath on Guptkashi Okhimath Gopeshwar motor road and passes though picturesque dense forests and green meadows. The journey is full of scenic beauty. From higher elevations on the way you get a close view of snow peaks. There are shops and good eating places at Chopta. You can get ponies for Tungnath from there. The hill sides are full of flowers and medicinal herbs.

The Tungnath temple is built after Katyuri style of architecture. The arms of Shiva are worshipped here.

Chandrashila is 3 km from the temple on a still higher elevation and you get a very close and wide view of the Himalayan peaks on its east and west and a wide view of the sub Himalayas far to the south.

15

Tungnath

The temple of Tungnath is on the highest elevation in the Himalayas. It is at the height of 3680 meters above sea level. The temple is 8 km from Chopta which is a very tough climb. Chopta is 30 km from Ukhimath on Guptkashi-Ukhimath-Gopeshwar motor road and passes through picturesque dense forests and green meadows. The journey is full of scenic beauty. From higher elevations on the way you get a close view of snow peaks. There are shops and good eating places at Chopta. You can get ponies for Tungnath from there. The hill sides are full of flowers and medicinal herbs.

The Tungnath temple is built after Katyuri style of architecture. The arms of Shiva are worshipped here.

Chandrashila is 1½ km from the temple on a still higher elevation and you get a very close and wide view of the Himalayan peaks on its east and west, and a wide view of the sub-Himalayas far to the south.

16

The Urgam Valley

An early snowfall makes the higher regions of the Himalayas very cold in December and January. The first week of January of 1956 had brought with it some rain in Joshimath but no snowfall. The high alpine meadows of Auli and the surrounding peaks were however covered in thick snow and appeared sparkling white from our garden. The farmers in the lower reaches were waiting to see their fields covered in snow. A heavy snowfall meant a bumper Rabi crop and proved useful for the fruit trees. The crops shoot up vigorously after the thaw and the soil retains moisture for a long time.

I went out on a tour of villages along the Alaknanda and Urgam valley. I reached Helang 11km from Joshimath, visited the neighboring Dungra and Saloor villages and halted at Helang. The next morning I left for Urgam valley ten kilometers west of Helang, across Alaknanda. B. N. Joshi (Assistant Development Officer, Social Education) was with me. The path descends down to Animath where there is an ancient temple of Bridhbadri, one of the five Badri temples. The others are Yogbadri at Pandukeshwar, Dhyanbadri at Urgam, Adibadri and finally, the main Badrinath temple. Bridhbadri has good fertile land with a small orange garden. It is said that in long past, devotees lived and worshiped here in their old age, because of its comparatively warm climate and peaceful atmosphere.

The only link to the Urgam valley over the Alaknanda was through a precariously laid out bridge. A pair of narrow hemp-ropes with matted railings rested on thick ropes anchored to rocks on either side of the narrow gorge. Only one person could pass over it at a time. The bridge would swing over the roaring river as one passed and this adrenalin pumping experience was a thrill for the adventure minded.

We climbed over a barren rocky hill and reached Salana village. The villagers welcomed and requested us to rest. I felt thirsty and asked for water. A lady standing at a distance said, "We can offer whatever we have except water. We have to cover a long distance down to a stream to fetch water for our family and cattle". She, however, went inside her house and brought a jar full of water.

"Is there any source from where water can be tapped for the village?" I asked.

"Yes sir", replied one of them. "It is quite far up in the forest".

"Are you ready to go to Pipalkoti to bring pipes and cement and start work?"

The villagers were more than willing and I quickly organized the initial spadework of finding the length of pipe and other construction material required for the project. I deputed some villagers to go to the godown at Pipalkoti and bring the required material.

"The project has to be completed in a fortnight", I told them and asked the V. L. W to complete necessary formalities and send the papers with a Gramsabha resolution.

This was the working method I followed in my village tours to speed up the projects where I found genuine need and people willing to work for it.

The scheme was completed within time and in my next visit I was happy to see a glow on the faces of the village people especially the women. The village tank was full of water and the prime need was fulfilled. I advised the ladies to utilize the time and energy they now had saved in growing vegetables and planting fruit trees.

The wide expanse of the two mile long valley opened before us as we reached the top of Salana village. It was an eye opening panorama. High mountains on three sides, covered with lush green forests, green wide fields and the Kalpganga River flowing on its eastern edge, the valley excelled in beauty and scenic splendour. It was an artist's dream. The northern slope was dotted with small houses with a temple on top.

Villagers led by the headman, Bhawan Singh Pradhan came to receive me with drums and garlands. This was a customary welcome by simple villagers during early years of Community Development. It was an expression of their aspirations and hopes from the new setup for a better life.

Situated at the height of 6,000ft above sea level, Urgam is a big village divided in several pockets. Nature has been bountiful to the valley and has bestowed it with fertile soil, abundance of water, rich pastures, dense forests and a very favorable climate for temperate fruits.

The holy temples of Vishnu and Shiva have made it a place for pilgrimage as well. The Dhyan Badri temple is dedicated to Vishnu. The Kalpashwar temple is dedicated to Shiva and is one of the five Kedars. The Dhyan Badri temple is in a prominent place above the village and gets some aid from the Badrinath temple for daily rituals. Kalpeshwar Dimri was then the priest of the temple. He told me that Urgam was once the Tapobhumi (place for penance) of great sages. It is named after Urgwa sage who performed great penance here. In the Puranic age Vanprasthis (people who get detached from their families and reside in the forests) lived in this valley. Atkinson says that a sect of Nagas called Urgas ruled this area hence it was called Urgam. The fertile Urgam valley was once the granary of Badrinath temple. A number of water mills which still exist used to grind wheat for the temple.

A meeting was held in the primary school ground. Problems of the village were discussed and a plan for their execution drawn out. The climate and soil of the valley is most suitable for apple and other temperate fruits and the rich pastures an asset for sheep breeding. Priority was given to both the programmes. I told them that Joshimath was soon to be connected by motor road and it would be easy for them to transport fruits and vegetables to Badrinath and towns on the pilgrim route. A ready market was at hand. I advised the sheep breeders to get Australian rams from Government Sheep Farm at Pipalkoti to improve the breed.

The Gram sabha resolved to construct a panchayat ghar and pave the village paths.

"We want to construct a tank to store water as the discharge of the spring from where we get our drinking water is low." Bhawan Singh said. He added, "The land where the tank is proposed belongs to a harijan and he is not willing to sell it or get another piece in exchange. This has created a problem."

The owner of the land was present in the meeting. I requested him to take some more land in the vicinity but he did not agree. On my second request he said, "How is it sir, officials who come to the village never visit our colony. You too came straight here. I will talk about this if you come to our colony".

"I am ready just now. Let us go" I replied.

"Please fix it for tomorrow any time that suites you".

"I will come in the morning", I told him.

"We have to go to Kalpeshwar in the morning", Bhawan Singh said softly.

"This is important, keep that for the afternoon".

I went to the colony next morning. Bhawan Singh and some other men were with me. The residents welcomed us. They had made sitting arrangement in the court yard of a double storied house. The house owner took me and Bhawan Singh to the verandah of the first floor. There were two chairs and a small table. He served us some fruits and biscuits.

"And where is the tea?", I said.

"Next time you visit," he said with a smile.

I relished the fruits served and came down to sit with the members of the colony in the courtyard. Urgam had an equal number of families of both the castes. I was pleased to know that they owned good land as well. I asked them their problems and assured them all help. The owner of the plot where the tank was proposed to be made came forward to give the land and was compensated by the village by giving him a better plot in exchange.

"Let there be a congenial atmosphere in the village", I said, "We all should live like a family. We do address the members of harijan families as uncle, grandfather, brother, sister according to their age. In my village it was an age long custom". The meeting ended in a cordial atmosphere.

We visited Kalpnath in the afternoon. It is in a cave under a huge rock on the left bank of The Kalpa Ganga. There is a Shiva Lingam and the matted hair of Lord Shiva is worshipped.

I went to Village Bharki two km from kalpnath on top of a high ridge It is a difficult walk and there is a local saying 'Saoo din Urgam ek din Bharki" (100 days in Urgam and one day at Bharki). People presumably visited this village once in a blue moon!

V. N. Joshi organized a youth club in the village. An energetic young man was elected president. They decided to stage a cultural programme in the night. A big fire was lit in a spacious ground and lighting arrangements were made. There was a very good gathering. Men, women, young and old came well dressed, protected against cold and sat in a circle leaving space for the dancers.

Women came in their traditional dress which is different from that in the lower mountains. They wear a long black woolen garment called Lawa. It is shorter in length than a saree and woven by the village weavers with thin woolen yarn spun locally. Ladies wrap it around the body and fasten both ends by a knot or a safety pin. This keeps their arms free to work. A full sleeve waist coat is worn over the lawa and the waist is kept tight with a long white cloth. The head is covered with a cotton scarf. This dress protects them from cold and the wearing style gives them a smart look being easy for daily work.

They were decked with silver and gold jewellery. Common jewellery worn was, a thick round silver necklace called Hasuli round the neck, silver or gold ear rings called Murkhulas, a gold ring on the nose and silver bangles on the wrists. The jewellery is given to them at the time of their marriage and is a social status symbol.

The function started with the beating of drums. Joshi himself was a good drummer. He slung the drum over his shoulder and led the group of dancers. He started with a popular devotional song.

"Kailashu ka Bhola Mahadeva teela dharu boola". Hail to thee, Mahadeva! The great God among gods; Immutable, passionless, free from anger, avarice, pride and easily approachable. The god who has his abode in Kailash, the most beautiful snow peak of the Himalaya. Singing the song and beating drums in perfect rhythm, the dance was a reflection of the pure and simple joys of the village people. This was followed by several other folk songs and dances. The gala came to a joyous close at midnight.

Three days of my wonderful stay in Urgam valley were fruitful and enjoyable. Bhawan Singh was with me all the time. He impressed me with his simplicity and sincerity. Bhawan Singh was an image of humility and humbleness.

He came to see me off and requested for another visit at an early date. I assured them and we were on way to Joshimath.

During my stay of three years at Joshimath, I visited Urgam valley and the distant Dumuk and Kalgot villages many times. It is half a century now that I saw the village last. I hear the valley is producing lot of apple and other fruits and if true, one of my dreams is fulfilled. The hemp rope bridge which served the older generation must be a thing of the past. The primary school may have been upgraded. These are all my imaginings but whatever the change, my mind still has the same old image of the serene Urgam valley lush green, enchanting and home to simple fun loving village people. It is forever imprinted in my mind.

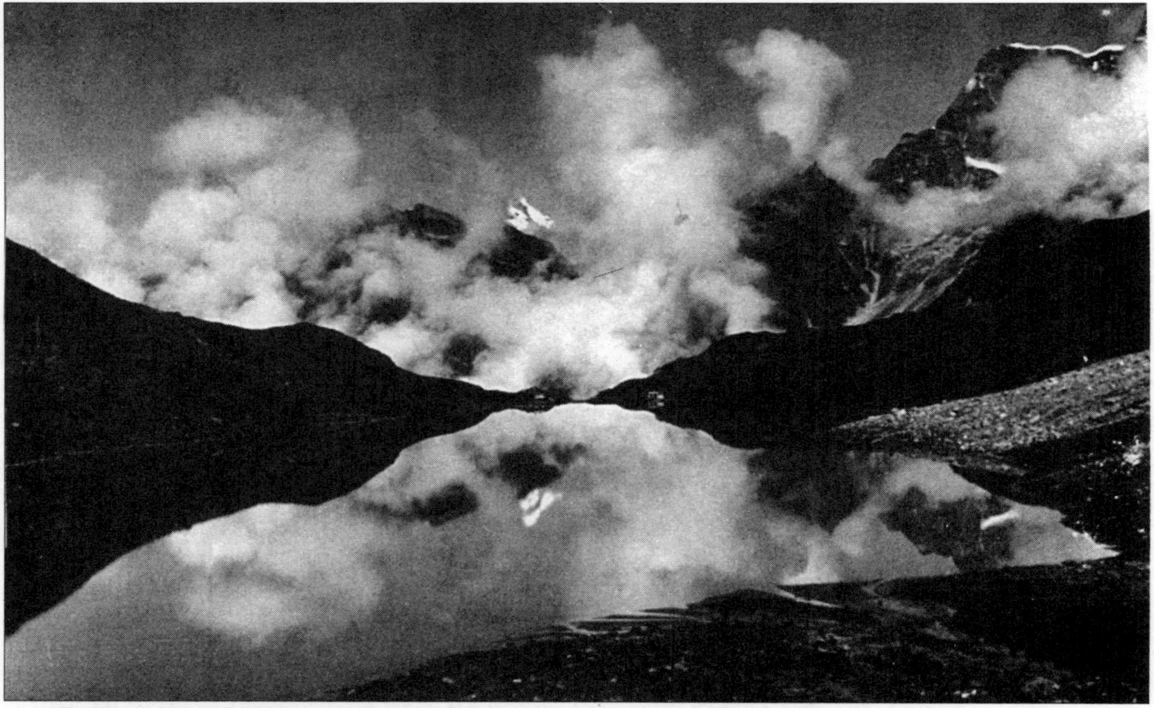

HEMKUND LOKPAL, REFLACTION OF NILKANTH PEAK IN THE LAKE, 1956

17

The Valley of Flowers

There were good rains followed by snowfall in Joshimath in the third week of January. I was working in my office on a cold and overcast afternoon. The room was made cosy by the burning charcoal in the fireplace. Pratap Singh Mehta, a journalist and businessman from Pandukeshwar, entered my room. We had met earlier when I was at Pandukeshwar for a day in December. Fair, young with blue eyes, Mehta had a pleasing personality.

"Take a seat Mehta", I said.

"How do you like the place," Mehta asked taking the chair close to the fire place.

"Immensely, what would you like to have-tea or coffee?"

"Coffee will be nice. I have come from Pandukeshwar and am a bit tired. You must have by now seen a lot of this area, I believe."

"Yes, I have covered a number of villages. I came from Urgam two days back. The splendid valley and its people have captivated me. It is the most picturesque place I have been to so far."

"You have yet to see many places of exquisite beauty. By the way, have you heard of the Valley of Flowers?"

"Valley of Flowers. What do you mean? Do the people grow just flowers and no grains or fruits? I am hearing the name for the first time."

"You have come from a valley inhabited and cultivated by human beings. I am talking of a valley which is Nature's garden, where flowers grow and bloom on their own. I have been there twice. It is a paradise and simply charming."

I got interested. "Tell me all about it; I am keen to go there at the earliest."

"Govindghat which is seven miles from here on way to Badrinath is the gateway to the Bhyundar Valley on the left bank of the Alaknanda. Valley of Flowers is 12 miles up from there." Mehta sipped the hot coffee and continued, "Legend says that Hanuman took sanjeewani herb from Dronagiri and Laxman who was lying unconscious on the battle field of Lanka was saved. The Gods expressed their happiness by showering celestial flowers over the Himalayas. It is these flowers which have been blooming all over Himalayas, particularly in valleys like the Valley of Flowers and alpine meadows. Bhyundar is the last village of the valley. The local people knew about this valley since long and brought Braham Kamal, a beautiful lotus-like flower from there to worship Lord Shiva. It is believed to be the most sacred offering to him.

Mehta paused for a while, took a sip of coffee and said, "It was Frank Smythe, the renowned mountaineer who explored the valley and brought it on the world map. Smythe climbed the Kamet peak (25,447 ft.) in 1931. He returned by Bhyundar pass (16,688 ft.) with the intention of exploring the mountainous region. Trudging the precipitous, rocky terrain he could never imagine that a pleasant surprise awaited him. He was bewitched when suddenly he stepped into this valley and found himself surrounded by many varieties of beautiful flowers. He forgot all his fatigue, pain and cold and camped there for two days. He named it the' Valley of Flowers.' He was so much enamored that he made a second visit to the enchanting valley in 1937, stayed for four months, roamed in the valley and scaled some of the neighboring peaks. He collected seeds, bulbs, tubers and plants and took them to England."

I listened to Mehta with rapt attention.

"The valley must be snow bound now. I will go as soon as the snow melts."

"Yes it is snow bound till April. The best time to go there is in July and August when the valley is in full bloom."

Mehta stayed with me for an hour. We talked about development programmes being taken up in the block.

I got busy with my work and the thought of the valley receded to the background.

It was the month of May. My two days stay at Badrinath in the first week animated my spirits. I met Mehta at Badrinath where he had a shop and was reminded of the Valley of Flowers.

"The valley must be free from snow," I asked. "I intend to go there."

"It is too early," he said, "you will find no flowers."

"Well, the valley is there and besides I have to visit village Bhyundar."

Mehta smiled and I left for the valley with Rameshwar Bhandari V. L. W (village level worker) of the area.

We reached Govindghat at two in the afternoon, crossed the Alaknanda by an old suspension bridge and climbed over the ridge. The path passed through a sparse forest. Covering a distance of three km we reached Pulna, a small village and the winter retreat of Bhyunder village four kilometers up the valley. Nandan Singh Pradhan of the Gram Sabha welcomed us and made arrangement for our night's stay.

The villagers assembled in the night and I discussed their problems. The Pradhan told me that they did not have a school in their village. I assured them that I would contact the Chairman of the District Board and get a primary school sanctioned at the earliest. I asked them to arrange some housing for the school till the time a new building could be constructed. Rameswer suggested that the village had recently constructed a panchayat ghar in Bhyunder with aid from the block and the school could run there for the present. On my return to Joshimath I requested Shridhar Azad the Chairman of District Board to sanction a primary school for Bhyunder and appoint a teacher immediately. Azad was kind enough to send a teacher and the school started functioning.

Their second demand was for a wooden bridge over the rivulet in Bhyunder. I inspected the site next day and told the pradhan to start the work.

We left for Bhyunder and Valley of Flowers early next morning. It was now a gradual climb through a dense pine forest. On a higher altitude there were oak, rhododendron and other deciduous trees. The rhododendrons were in full bloom. They grow to a height of ten thousand feet. With increase in altitude, the flowers change their color from red to pink and then to white. Above a height of 9,000ft the tall trees take the form of bushes and the flowers get light blue. We rested at Bhyunder for an hour, had our lunch and left for Ghangaria 7km up in the valley.

Situated at a height of 9,000ft above sea level, Ghangaria is a lovely camping spot full of tall deodar trees and is the base for visitors to the Valley of Flowers and pilgrims to the holy Hemkund Lokpal. A forest rest house was the only place to stay then. The place had few visitors in those days. A mountain track bifurcated into two with the left going to the Valley of Flowers and the right to Lokpal We followed the left path, crossed the Laxman Ganga that comes from Lokpal. It is a gradual climb and the conifers started to replace the deciduous trees. We were getting closer to the snow line. The fresh winter snow had started melting and was sliding down the slopes making it difficult to walk. Clouds were gathering and we were afraid it might rain. Nandan Sing said that at times there was snow fall in May as well.

The valley opened gradually as if hesitant to reveal its beauty. Soon we reached the top of the ridge and the full panoramic view was before us. It is a large valley more than six miles long and two miles wide with a magnificent backdrop of Rataban peak far towards the East. The sight was far more enchanting than I had imagined.

We were now at a height of more than 11,000 ft above sea level. It was cold and the month of May was like February in Joshimath. I sat on a rock overlooking the valley and was reminded of a famous line from Shelley's "Ode to the West Wind", "If winter comes, can spring be far behind."

Winter had gone and it was spring time in the high Himalayan reaches. The valley was waking from its long slumber and resurging. The wet spongy turf was pulsating with life, pushing up myriads of shoots to bloom and spread a carpet of beautiful flowers in the meadows. Down below was a dense bushy forest of rhododendrons with buds ready to burst and bloom into snow white flowers. The Pushpawati River was flowing with an indistinct murmur close by. Its right bank was covered with a thick forest of silver birch, a nice habitat for musk deer. The valley abounds in beautiful birds especially the Himalayan monal, a big bird with colored plumage like that of a peacock.

There was absolute calm. A crow was making its lonely flight over the meadows. I noticed a white spot at some distance below.

"What is that white thing Nandan Singh", I asked.

"It is the grave of Margaret Lagge, an English lady", he replied. "She was here years back to collect flowers, seeds, bulbs and tubers. She slipped from a high slope while collecting the samples and succumbed to her injuries. I still remember the day when a porter came running to our village from the valley and gave the sad news of her death. The headman went to Joshimath to inform the patwari and the police. The magistrate at Chamoli was also informed. The government sent a message to her family in England. Her sister requested the Indian Government to bury the body in the valley. She came here after a year and built that small memorial. We went to the grave. The following epitaph was inscribed on a white stone.

"I will lift mine eyes unto the hills

From where cometh my help."

The eyes of her spirit may be looking at these beautiful hills and meadows which had attracted her from far across the seven seas. Her body it seemed had merged with the valley to continue blooming each summer.

"We are getting late", Nandan Singh said. "Let us go and reach Bhyunder before it is dark."

I paid my respects to the departed soul and bade good bye to the valley.

We hurried back and reached Nandan Singh's house at Bhyunder just before dark. I had a good night's rest in a warm cosy room of his house and was back in Joshimath the next day.

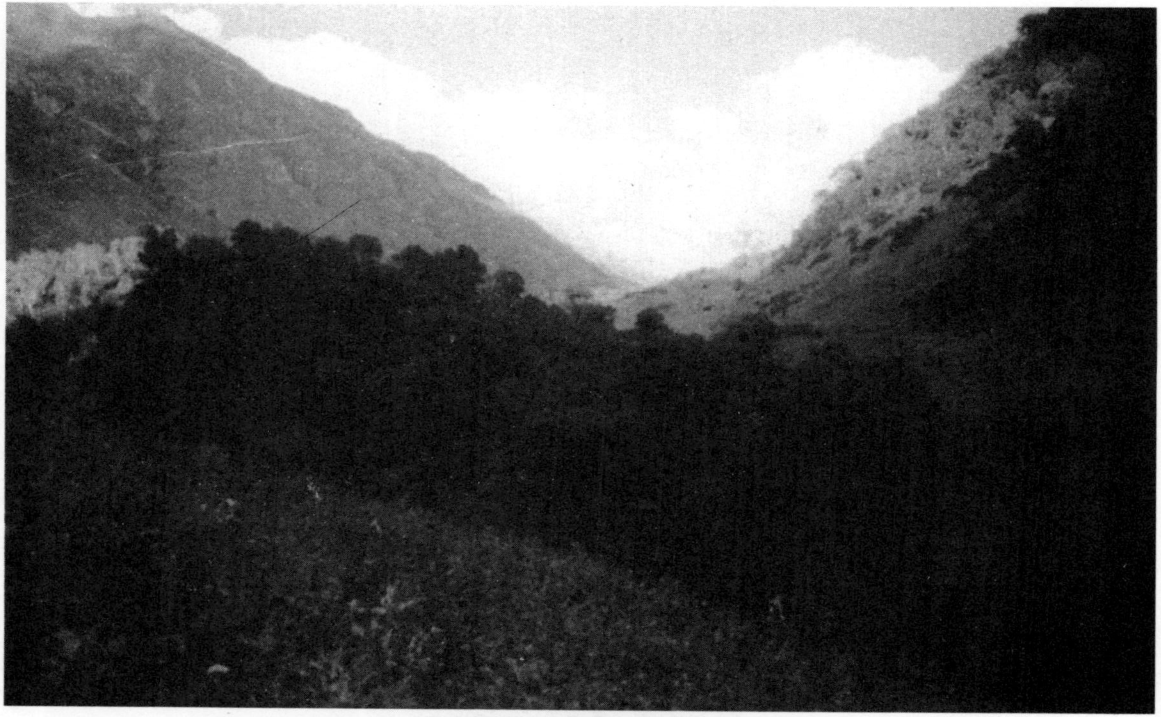

VALEEY OF FLOWERS

18

The Valley in Bloom

May, June and July were very busy months. Soon after my return from the Valley of Flowers I toured all the villages including Dronagiri in the Niti valley. Niti is 45 miles from Joshimath and is10, 000 ft above sea level.

I visited the Valley of Flowers a second time in the last week of August 1956. Mr. Ram Sahay, the Divisional Commissioner and Mr Bagchi visited Joshimath block. The Commissioner inspected many development projects and addressed a youth camp that we had organized at Helang. He was satisfied with the tempo and pace of development work in the block and expressed his pleasure to Bagchi.

"We are going to the Valley of Flowers tomorrow", he told me, and "I hope to see some development projects in that valley. Tell me what will you show me?"

"It will be better if you see them first", I replied.

We left for the valley and stayed at Govind Ghat Gurudwara that night. Usha Pati Bhatt, Assistant Development Commissioner of border area met us at Govind Ghat. The next day we reached Bhyunder at one in the afternoon. The villagers welcomed us. Nandan Singh took Sahay to the panchayat ghar constructed four months back. The recently sanctioned primary school was functioning in that building. Small boys and girls garlanded Sahay. I showed the newly constructed bridge. The Commissioner was pleased and praised the villagers for the interest taken by them. He asked the villagers, who had assembled there to plant fruit trees and cultivate vegetables. The Valley of Flowers and Lokpal are going to attract a lot of tourists and pilgrims in the near future and the village will have a ready market.

We left for Ghangaria after tea and reached at five in the evening. The Commissioner stayed in the forest rest house and the rest of the officers in tents pitched in the compound.

The next day we left for Hemkund Lokpal. It was a cloudy morning and as we climbed, it started raining. At an altitude of 14,000ft above sea level Lokpal is five miles from Ghangaria. We had hardly covered two miles when there was a heavy downpour. The umbrellas were of little help. We got wet and it was cold. It would be worse at that height, we thought. We turned back and reached Ghangaria in an hour. Fire was lit and all of us warmed ourselves and had hot tea.

"Let us discuss the border area development plan," the Commissioner said. He asked Mr. Bhatt to take out the papers. The Commissioner reviewed the progress made so far and a discussion on proposed plans followed. Among other plans there was a new proposal for the cultural development of the border areas.

"The borders are a treasury of folk songs and dances that need to be preserved and encouraged," Bhatt said.

I related my experiences of the kisan mela and said that the Gopi dance of village Lata and Bagdwal dance of Pandukeshwar had been a great attraction. The scheme for cultural development was sanctioned by the government after some months and was a success. We had lively and fruitful discussions that day.

The sky was clear and sunny when we left for the Valley of Flowers at eight the next morning.

After a nice walk of three miles we reached the valley at ten. The valley was in full bloom. It was a feast for the eyes. It looked magnificently different than my last visit. Vegetation which I had seen in its early stage was now in full youth, vibrating with life and spreading its radiance all-around. The super gardener had adorned the valley with flowers of different colors-white, yellow, red and blue in a magnificent arrangement. It was a marvelous display of nature. The flowers seemed countless-much like "Wordsworth's daffodils". We walked cautiously to avoid crushing them under our feet. Most of the flowers mentioned in Smythe's book were there but we missed the Himalayan poppy that Smythe has named 'Queen of the Himalayan flowers'. We searched every where but could not find it. I climbed over the hill and was lucky to spot some of the blue poppies blooming in the crannies. The beautiful flowers were fluttering in the soft breeze, whispering to me, "here we are, aloof from the crowd below, seated on our majestic throne." What a marvelous creation of God? A few lines of Lord Tennyson's poem "Flowers in the Crannied Wall" came to my mind.

"Little flower but if I could understand

What you are, root and all, and all in all

I should know what god and man is."

I was lost in the mystery of creation and wondered, "Who created these beauties, gave them form and life." People, down below, plucked flowers, making beautiful bouquets. I stopped myself from plucking poppy the queen of flowers. Let her reign in her territory I thought.

Each one had made a bouquet. The sun had moved to the West. We did not know how the hours had passed in this playground of the Gods. The time for departure from the valley had come and we started on our way back.

On our return to Ghangaria, a big table was brought out and flowers were displayed with names labeled according to Smythe's book.

Visit to Hemkund Lokpal

We were to leave for Pandukeshwar next morning. The thought of missing a visit to Lokpal was pinching me. I decided to make a hurried trip early in the morning and asked Rameshwar Bhandari to accompany me. We took a torch and left at four in the morning. It was still dark. I was young and fond of climbing. We reached Lokpal at 6. 30 in the morning, covering a distance of 5 miles. It was an enchanting sight. A celestial lake at the height of 14,000 ft. above sea level, it was an excellent handiwork of nature, skillfully carved out and resting in the lap of seven snow peaks.

Legend says that Laxman, the younger brother of Ram performed penance here. There was then an old dilapidated temple on the right bank where people from neighboring villages and from Niti valley came for worship. The place is also sacred to the Sikhs. According to their holy scriptures Guru Govind Singh meditated here in his past life. The Sikhs erected a nice gurudwara and thousands of Sikh pilgrims visit this holy shrine.

The water of the lake is crystal clear and the reflection of Neelkanth peak in the far West glowingly reflects in the transparent water on a clear day. The peak was covered with light fog and I had to wait for fifteen minutes to take a clear photograph of the lake with Neelkanth in the background. I took a dip in the holy lake and felt rejuvenated. I bowed to the gurudwara and the laxman temple and hurried back to catch the party at Ghangaria.

This was my last visit to the mesmerizing Bhyundar Valley and Hemkund Lokpal which in those days was visited by just a few enthusiastic mountaineers, explorers and pilgrims. I now learn that thousands of tourist and pilgrims go there each year. The path is littered with plastic bags, bottles and other garbage even though the valley has been declared a National Park and a recognized world heritage, I am sure that the wonder of the place some forty years back is no more.

The Laxman temple has been renovated and a big gurudwara has been erected.

I do not know if the simple village people living in the valley have improved their lot or are still in poverty, serving tea and snacks and giving a ride to affluent tourists on their mules.

The valley and the lake will ever remain in my mind a paradise on earth.

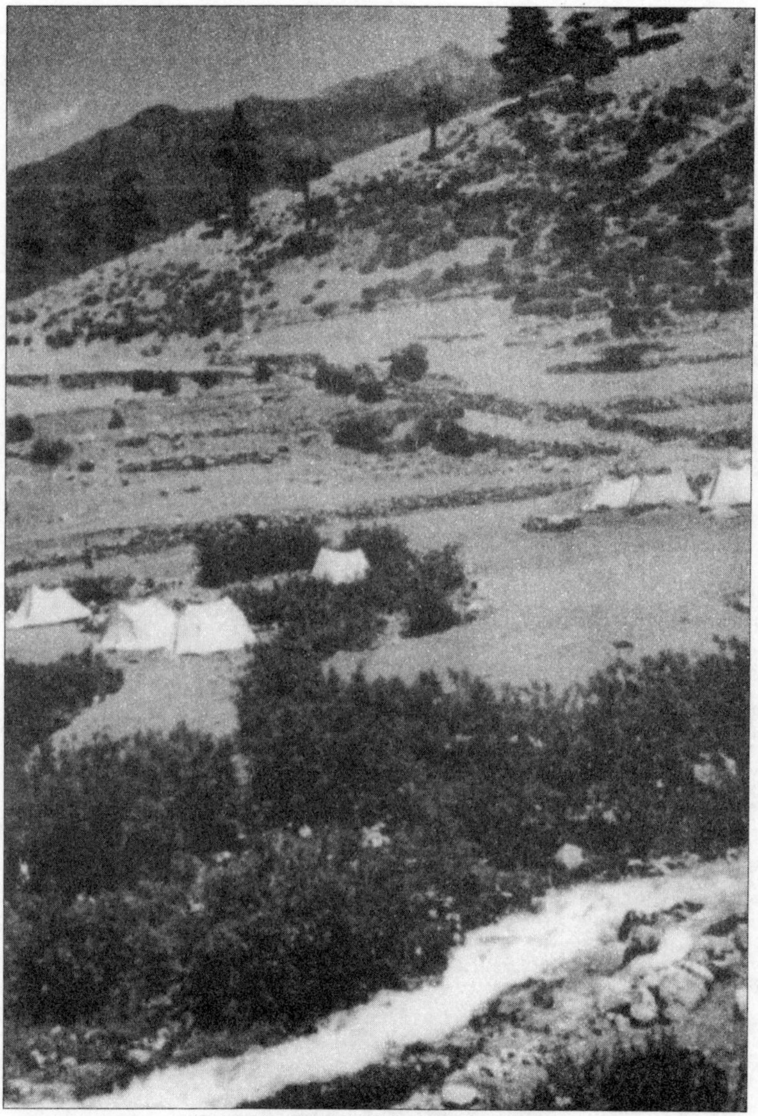

CAMP SITE MALARI, 1956

19

The Niti Valley

Joshimath is at its best in May and June. Bidding spring adieu the long summer sun fills the hills with its warmth. Evenings get cloudy and occasional rains bring freshness in the air. Apple, apricot, pear, plum, peach, cherry and walnut trees are laden with fruit. Rows of red roses bloom in gardens. The wild rose bushes along the paths and in shady corners are covered with bunches of small white flowers and scatter sweet perfume all around.

The Badrinath route is dotted with pilgrims. Men, women, young and old trudging their way to the holy shrine with immutable faith in Badri Vishal and many returning back from their pilgrimage happy and contented after a darshan of the deity, is an interesting sight.

Joshimath then was a small place. The houses, built of mud and stone with slate roofs gave it a quaint look. Standing in the midst of the concrete jungle, that the place is today, it is indeed hard to imagine the old-world charm of the yester-years. Even the Auli heights have not been spared. I remember I would climb up the virgin Auli-Gorson alpine slopes nine to ten thousand feet above sea level on Sundays, all alone, and wander in the quietude of the mountains lending my ears to the unheard music of the dazzling snow peaks. I would listen to the melodies of birds and songs of the rivulets as they gurgled down the mountain slopes.

With green meadows, the snow peaks at a distance and the blue sky, it was truly a heaven on earth.

I was back from a fruitful tour of Badrinath, Mana and Bhyundar valley. The time seemed right to visit Niti valley, a trip I was looking forward to, since joining the block. I was keen to see the villages of the high valley and meet people who migrate to lower regions in winter and go back to the valley in summer, traders who shuttle between Kotdwara-Ramnagar mandis near the Himalayan foot hills and the Tibetan Plateau, the roof of the world, roughly covering a distance of six to seven hundred miles a year with merchandise loaded on sheep and goats.

Most of the migrating families had returned from their winter resorts in villages near Chamoli, Nandprayag and Karanprayag while some were on way. They move with their household belongings loaded on ponies, goats, and bullocks. Their journey starts at daybreak and ends at ten in the morning, leaving enough time for the cattle to graze.

The Niti valley is inhabited by two classes of people- the Tolchas and the Marchas. The Tolchas live in the villages of Lata, Rinni, Juwa, Jugjug, Long, Fagty, Jumma, Jhelum, Dronagiri and Malari. This is the lower half of the valley. The marchas live in Kailashpur, Bampa. Farkia, Gamsali and Niti which is the upper half, while some marchas also live in Malari.

I prepared for the long tour which would take about ten days. Some members of the field staff said that it was too early but I was impatient. V. N. Joshi (ADO) volunteered to accompany me. He was a person who was ever ready for any duty. He could be put on any road with any load.

On a sunny May morning we left for the Niti valley, stopping at Bargaon and Tapoban on the way. Situated at a distance of nine miles from Joshimath, Tapoban is a small village on the left bank of Dhauli and known for its hot water spring. There is a cool water spring as well and you can mix both the waters to make it Luke warm for a comfortable bath. It is said that the Katyuri kings shifted their capital from Joshimath to this place in the tenth century A. D to have a better control over their kingdom which extended beyond Niti. There are some old temples near the village. The temple of Bhavishy badri is about four miles up in Subhai village. Tapoban is on the famous Joshimath-Kunwari Ramni-Gwaldum trekking route.

Our first halt was at Lata that is twelve miles from Joshimath and at a height of about 7,000. ft above sea level. Lata, Rini and Juwa are immutably permanent villages as they are not snow bound. Their main occupation is agriculture. Some hardy young men work as guides and porters for mountaineers and go with expeditions to Nanda Devi peak. The route passes through Lata along the Rishiganga river which originates from the Nanda Devi glacier.

There is an ancient temple of goddess Nanda Devi on top of the village. It is a Shakti peeth (possessing primal power) and is well honored in the district. The pujari told me that most of the mountaineers come here to pray for a safe and successful expedition to Nanda Devi peak.

Nanda Devi National Park and the Peak

River Dhauli divides the Central Himalayas into two great ranges. There is the Badrinath range on the Northwest and the Nanda Devi range on the Northeast. The flanks of Nanda Devi which include a huge area consisting of several high peaks, glaciers, alpine meadows, rivers, dense forests and gorges was made a sanctuary in 1939 and awarded the status of a national park in 1982. Covering an area of 650sq km, it is the most picturesque and spectacular part of the central Himalayas. Its unique physiography and biotic resources impressed UNESCO and a 5,800sq km Biosphere Reserve was declared as one of the world heritage site in 1988 to protect the region's fragile ecosystem. The park consists of a cluster of many peaks enshrouded with religious sanctity, myth and mystery. The major peaks in the National Park are Nanda Devi (one of the highest peaks of India at 25,645ft), Nanda Ghunti (20,700ft), Nanda Kot (22,530ft), Trishul I (23,406), Trisul II (23,490ft), Trisul III (22,360ft), Nandakhat (6611meters, Devistan 6678 meters, Kalanka 6931 meters, Rishi Pahar 6931 meters and Mangraon 6765 meters above sea level.

I have watched the Himalayas with absolute devotion. They are not just monolithic columns of granite rocks covered with perpetual snow but ensouled with divinity. Our sages have personified them as gods and goddesses and named them Gauri Shanker, Narayan, Shivling, Srikanth, and goddess Nanda Devi and Gauri. They are the paths (Swarga Rohini) to heaven by one of which the Pandavas are said to have ascended to heaven.

Nanda Devi is the manifestation on earth of Nanda Bhagwati, the goddess of bliss. Being the pride of Himalaya it is matchless in beauty and grandeur. I have watched her peerless beauty from the alpine heights of Gorson, 6 miles from Joshimath. Towering far above the rest of her courtiers, the queen stands with regal detachment with all her royal paraphernalia. There is Nandakot, her royal fort, Nandakhat her royal bed, Nandaghunti her regal veil and Panchchuli the five cooking ovens which serve her royal kitchen. Three peaks of Trisul, the mighty trident of Shiva, stand as eternal guards.

On a sudden glance from an opening in the Rishiganga valley she was awe inspiring but charmingly majestic as I continued my gaze. She communes directly and you are at once captivated by her divine aura.

Nanda Devi is the native goddess of both Garhwal and Kumaon. Loving daughter of the Himalayas, she was born and brought up in the Himalayan heights where she grew up into a matchless beauty on earth. She performed great austerities and was married to Shiva at Trijuginarayan. This great occasion is celebrated throughout the hills on the auspicious day of Nanda-ashtami, which falls in October.

The biggest celebration is held at village Nauti, 14 km from Karnprayag in Chamoli district after every twelve years. A seventeen day long Nanda Raj yatra (pilgrimage) starts from her natal place to the abode of her husband Shiva in distant snow peak. Lakhs of people participate in the festival. A four-horned ram takes birth every twelfth year. The ram leads the procession and carries the belongings of the goddess all the way. The goddess is given a tearful parting by young and old women who assemble here in large number. They weep when the doli of their beloved daughter departs from her parental home.

The goddess is taken in a silver palanquin. The procession passes through the alpine pastures of Bedani and takes the high precipitous snow covered route. It ends at Homkund near the foot of Trisul peak where the goddess is worshipped with great reverence and rejoicing. The four horned ram is let loose. The ram climbs up the snow peak all alone and finally disappears. The party returns and waits for another twelve years for the next yatra.

May the ancient legend of Nanda Bhagwati continue to live in countless fairs held throughout the hills of Garhwal and Kumaon. Nanda, the primordial power of Shiva; the immutable and immortal goddess comes down to earth as a bride after every twelve years. She is loved by mortals as their own beloved daughter and sent to her husband's abode with wet eyes. Nanda, the consort of Shiva! May she continue to be a bride, ever young and beautiful and bless us all?

The stay at Lata was a satisfying one. I advised the young boys to become expert mountaineers and good guides, and earn a good living like the Sherpa of Nepal as a number of expeditions went to Nanda Devi peak each year. Some of the young who had gone with the expeditions related their interesting experiences. Lata is known for its special folk dance the "Gopi nritya" in which both the male and female members of the village take part. It is a weeklong festival held in the month of April. I witnessed this function. The male members of the party took an active part in block level cultural functions and won prizes. I took the party to the Gaucher fair in November 1956. Their performance was highly appreciated and rewarded.

After the company of the people of Lata, we resumed our march the next morning. I met some villagers of Juwa a small village on the bank of Dhauli. They told me that the women folk had to walk a long distance to get water from the river. The shortage of water is a perennial one in most villages in Garhwal, home to the mighty rivers. The shortage of water was overcome by providing a pipeline to bring water from distant springs.

A foot track passes along the river bank to Surainthota, five miles from Lata, where the valley narrows down, with huge perpendicular cliffs on either side. Dhauli is quite turbulent here. Dashing against big boulders, it descends down with roaring sound.

While writing these lines after a long time today, I am reminded of a flash flood. It was clear and sunny on 3 July 1957. Usha Pati Bhatt, Assistant Development Commissioner of border areas was on a tour of Niti. As we were passing along this part of the road I saw Dhauli flooded with muddy water carrying a number of green deodar trees with it. It was an unusual phenomenon. We were at Surainthota at twelve noon and had planned to reach Jumma, nine miles ahead for the night. Everyone was at a loss about the turbulence. The water would stop completely for fifteen to twenty minutes and roar down again with greater speed and volume, rolling down boulders and trees with its powerful currents. This furious dance of the river continued the whole day. The bridge connecting the valley was not safe to cross and it was probable that the road on the other side had been washed away.

We stayed in a one-room rest house. At ten in the night a school teacher came to inform us that the river had started to erode its bank and the rest house being close to the river was in danger. He requested us to shift to the school building, which was half a k. m. up on a safe place. Mr Bhatt who was engrossed in a book was not inclined to leave his comfortable bed at this odd hour of the night. He proposed to take turns at sleeping and was to be the first on vigil, and was to wake me at about two in the morning. The teacher took leave and I went to sleep. I got up with a start. It was four in the morning and the roaring sound of the river seemed to come from the very courtyard. On rushing out I saw the river just a few yards away. Mr Bhatt meanwhile was deep in slumber. He had not woken me before he went to sleep. I shook him awake and we both ran to a safe place. It was our luck that the river did not strike the rest house or we would have been washed away. At about eight in the morning the suspension bridge that was the only link for the Niti valley was washed away.

We decided to return to Joshimath. We had hired two mules to carry our luggage. Just a mile ahead the road had been washed away. Padam Singh, the local muleteer was well acquainted with the terrain. He guided us and took us up a rocky hillock and clearing the undergrowth made way. He had great difficulty in pushing the loaded mules across the cliffs. After an arduous walk over wild unfrequented mountain trails we reached Tapovan late in the evening; fatigued and in need of rest. It took us nearly ten hours to cover a distance of nine miles. We thanked our stars for the safe home coming. At Joshimath we were informed by a wireless message from Niti that one of the glaciers of Dronagiri region slipped down the Dronagiri River and brought with it a huge mass of debris and the uprooted deodar trees of a dense forest and had blocked Dhauli near Jumma. A four mile long lake was formed between Jumma and Kosha village which explained the intermittent flow of the river witnessed by us.

Coming back to my present tour, we reached Jhelum fourteen miles from Lata at six in the evening. Jhelum is a big village. The residents are mostly traders. Govind Singh Rana was the pradhan of the gram sabha. He welcomed us. We had already met at Joshimath before. A stout young man, Govind Singh was frank, impressive and full of life. He was a prominent trader of the valley and quite popular in Tibet. He told me that once the Tibetan government appointed him jongpen, (an administrative officer) of a district in Tibet. He showed me some presents, which he had received from the Tibetan Government of which he was very proud.

Next morning we visited Kosha, a small village three miles from Jhelum. The villagers wanted to construct a log bridge over a river. They completed it in three months.

There is a bridge over Dhauli near Kosha at Bhapkund. Crossing the bridge the road passes through a wooded hill. As I climbed up the hill, the view arrested my wandering gaze by its scenic splendour. There were meadows spotted with green juniper bushes scattered around and gentle graceful slopes with deodar trees lined up against the horizon. A sparkling rivulet running with its sweet murmuring made it an ideal place for camping. Some families moving to their village had pitched their white tents. I appreciated their sense of beauty in choosing this beautiful camping spot. It was a pleasant and refreshing walk through the meadows and as we crossed the ridge, Malari valley opened before us.

Situated at the eastern edge of a one-mile long and half a mile broad picturesque valley, Malari is the biggest village of this area. There are streams and high mountains on both the sides with snow on tops and in the ravines. With the Dhauli in the West and green deodar trees on the surrounding hills the village has a beautiful setting. The inhabitants are mostly Tolchas with just nine or ten Marcha families. There are extensive well-terraced fields, which grow potato, barley, chinna, phaper and some wheat. The villagers are good cultivators and take interest in farming. I wrote to Vivekanand Agriculture Research Farm at Almora and received some wheat seeds for high altitude area. The plants grew well but unfortunately early snowfall in the last week of September damaged the crop.

I met the villagers who are traders, farmers and sheep breeders. We discussed about improving the breed of sheep, improved farming and planting of some apple and other temperate fruit trees on a trial basis. The gramsabha wanted to construct a panchyatghar, which was approved by the Block Advisory Committee later. They completed it that year.

Malari village seems to have a prehistoric past as some ancient pottery from Stone Age era has been found in some graves along with human bones. After a night's stay we left for Bampa seven miles up on the bank of the Dhauli.

Bampa gave a deserted look, as the families had not arrived. We stayed in the rest house of P. W. D. The next day we visited Gamsali and Niti villages where the families had reached.

Gamsali is one mile from Bampa at an altitude of 10,317 feet above sea level. Situated on the right bank of the Dhauli, Gamsali is a big village with flat fields around the village, which grow barley, oats and phapra. A sheer vertical cliff rises behind the village. Towards the West, is a rugged valley which is scattered with huge boulders. A stream and high snow peaks complete this picturesqe setting. Smythe went through this valley to scale Kamet peak in 1931. Facing to the Southeast you get a beautiful view of this long valley and its dense green forests of deodar trees and view of snow clad peaks in the background. Deodar ends near Bampa and is replaced by birch and high altitude pine up to Niti. I went to the village, met the pradhan and Pan Singh, a prominent man of the valley. He wanted the junior high school Gamsali to be upgraded into high school. A resolution was passed by the Block Advisory Committee to upgrade the school and sent to the Education Department.

Niti Village

From Gamsali the road passes through a narrow gorge and opens up after two miles. Situated at an altitude of 11,461ft above sea level, Niti is the last village in the valley. It is four miles from Bampa and 45 miles from Joshimath. The houses are clustered at an extreme corner under the cliffs of a huge mountain. The village is on the left bank of Dhauli and the right bank is covered with birch and pine trees. Houses are built of mud and stones and roofed with deodar planks.

There are two passes from Niti to Tibet, the Niti pass and the Chor Hoti pass. The route to Niti pass starts from the village itself and to Chor Hoti pass from a point one mile to the south. Part of the village is prone to avalanches. In the year 1957 a heavy snowfall in the month of October caused big damage to life and property. We met Sri Uday Singh Rana, Pradhan Gram Sabha and several other villagers and returned to Bampa in the evening. After a stay of two nights at Bampa we came back to Malari for our onward journey to Dronagari village on the last leg of our tour.

20

Dronagiri Village and the Majestic Peak

Situated in a distant pocket of the valley, Southeast of Malari and East of Jhelum, Dronagari is a small village of about ninety hamlets perched on a mountain about 10,500ft high above sea level. A 14 miles long village path, winding through a dense deodar forest along Dronagari gad [river] links the village. We left Malari at eight in the morning and encountered some tough climb on way. We reached the village at three in the afternoon. Pathalya Dass, the VLW (village level worker) had informed us earlier that the families had reached the village but we found none. The VLW whom we had informed about our visit appeared after fifteen minutes. The villagers, he said were scared to hear that some government officials were coming from Joshimath. They have left for their fields or the jungles. He, however, could persuade the pradhan who came soon after. The pradhan, a young man stood with an inexpressive face. I tried to take him in confidence, went up to him and said, "We have come here to help you and not to embarrass or trouble anyone. Tell me frankly, what difficulties do you face in this remote village? We will try to solve them. Presently I have seen that the path to your village is in bad shape. There are no bridges over the river on way to this place."

"Yes sir", he replied. "No government servant has ever come to our village to help us. Long back during British Raj, English surveyors used to come here for survey work but they too never cared for the village. We want to improve the road and construct three wooden bridges but we have no means, no money to pay the wages of the masons and the carpenters."

"You start the work", I said. The bridges will be subsidized by the government and the subsidy will suffice for meeting the wages of the masons and the carpenters. The rest of the work will have to be done by the gramsabha with contributory labour.

The Pradhan seemed happy. He took us to his house. "I am sorry for the misunderstanding", he apologized. He entertained us with hot tea and boiled potatoes which were the need of the hour. On my next visit to the village in September that year I was delighted to see a road and the three bridges spanning over the sparkling river.

Nestled in the periphery of the majestic Dronagiri peak (23,531ft) of the epic Ramayan, Dronagiri became my favorite village which I visited twice each year of my stay in Joshimath. I loved the village, its surrounding pastures, the glaciers, the gigantic Dronagiri peak and above all the people who were poor, simple with little or no contact with the outside world and dependent upon their fields, cattle and sheep for living. Some young men with the traders went to Tibet. They grew good crop of potato, barley, phaper and chinna. There are extensive alpine pastures above the village and are known for their efficacious herbs. An old man told me that long ago he had worked with an English surveyor who was suffering from piles. One day the surveyor went out to ease himself. He used some grass instead of toilet paper and was miraculously cured of this ailment.

My next visit in September that year was memorable. Back from tour of Niti valley I was at Malari. Mohan Singh Rana, Village Level Worker had come with me to take his horse from Dronagiri where he had sent it for grazing in the pastures under the care of Nain Singh. Rana was very popular with the people of the valley, as he had previously worked as teacher in many schools. Khushal Singh Rawat, panchayat secretary of the area was also with me. Pradhan Malari told me that there was a shorter route for Dronagiri village, which though difficult as it passed through a high mountain, was worth trying. He offered to give a guide. I was tempted to explore a new area.

Three of us marched with the guide at eight in the morning. We had hardly walked a mile when we met some women digging out potatoes in their fields.

"Where are you going?" inquired an elderly lady.

"To Dronagiri village". I replied.

"Dronagiri? Who told you that this is the way?"

"The pradhan of your village," I said.

"This is a very difficult route. You will perish. Return back and take the main path".

"There is no going back, sister", I said, and we continued our march.

It was a beautiful area. There were long wide cultivated terraces and mountain brooks which provided abundant water. We walked on a gentle gradient for some distance. There was then a high mountain to climb. It was autumn and the grass on the mountain slopes was drying. I was fond of climbing but my companion Rana who was comparatively old could not keep pace with me. They both lagged far behind. At two in the afternoon I was up on the peak of the 16,000 ft. high mountain. The guide, a young man had followed me. I sat down to rest, looked at the sky, which was getting cloudy. The guide turned to me and said, "I have to go to Malari. It may rain." Pointing his finger to the Southeast he said, "Descend down to the other side, go beyond that distant hill and you will reach the village".

He handed over the packed lunch and hurried down. He gave me no time to understand his directions properly.

I tried to locate Rana and Rawat but there was no trace of them anywhere. I was alone at that height. It got cloudy and the wind was cold. I was afraid it might rain. I got worried about Rana and Rawat, who I thought, may have lost their way. After half an hour I spotted two small figures crawling like ants far below. I felt relieved. Clouds were moving fast. The two reached the top at three in the afternoon.

It was now a steep descent on the other side of the peak down to a stream about a mile. Stepping down was more difficult then climbing. We reached the stream and sat on the meadow for lunch. Some shepherds were there with their flock of sheep. They must be cooking meat, Rana said. He went to them and brought a bowl of hot soup. After a hurried lunch we started our march on a narrow goat track southeast. It became foggy and started drizzling. We had no umbrellas and there was no place to take shelter as it was a barren hill. After a mile the track branched off and we could not decide which way to follow. The rain continued. We got wet and it became very cold at that height. The fog reduced visibility. We lost the sense of direction and were not sure if we were following the right track. What will happen if the path leads us to a strange land in the night? Rawat, a tough guy came forward. "Follow me Sir", he said.

"Were you here before and are you sure of the way?" I was a bit irritated as is usual at high altitudes.

"No Sir, I have never come this way, I am just using my common sense."

There was no choice but to follow Rawat and we continued the march. Rana who was silent till now opened his mouth. "That lady was right Sir, I am going to perish if the rain does not stop and we do not reach the village".

"Don't lose heart Rana", I tried to give him strength.

We were at our wits end. All of us were terribly tired. It was getting dark and rain had stopped for the moment.

"Let us sit and rest our tired bones for a while", I said.

Suddenly a miracle happened. The sky on the Southeast cleared a bit and we saw a cluster of houses at a distance. We rejoiced and felt our strength returning even as our spirits soared. We stood up in prayer and thanked God. I praised Rawat for his common sense which in the circumstances had proved uncommon.

We now stepped forward on our march and soon were on a path that led us to the village. It was dark when we reached Nain Singh's house. He was surprised to see us arriving at this odd hour. He gave us a very warm welcome and took us to his room where a good fire was burning. We warmed ourselves and dried our wet clothes. A cup of hot tea and boiled potatoes gave us strength to move. Nain Singh arranged for our stay in the school building.

After the day's tough and tiresome journey in wet and cold weather I had a sound sleep in the warm cosy room of the school. The morning was cloudless and sunny. It was pleasant to sit out in the warmth of the morning sun. The villagers gathered and sat near me. By now we were quite close. Some young men who had gone with the traders to Tibet were back with their meager earnings. The shepherds were on way to the village with their flocks back from pastures. The crops were good, especially potato which is a major crop of the village. The bridges, which I had asked them to construct during my last visit, were completed long back and the pradhan told me that he had received the aid from the block office. I asked the villagers to pave the village lanes and keep the village clean.

The alpine pastures of Dronagiri are a treasure of rare and costly medicinal herbs, which only grow in high altitudes. There was no proper plan for their extraction and preservation. If planned properly it could be a good subsidiary source of income for the village. The government is now paying attention to this invaluable treasure of the Himalayas.

I was keen to go to the pastures, the glaciers and watch the grandeur of the magnificent Dronagiri peak from the nearest point approachable. Three young men offered to guide me and we left after breakfast. We passed through extensive pastures. With autumn the plants had started withering. It was all a bed of beautiful flowers last month, the young men told me. We climbed up the glaciers; there are seven of them. The majestic Dronagiri was now in full view glittering in the morning sun against a clear blue sky. After Nanda Devi, the undisputed goddess of the Himalayas, Dronagari is the finest peak of this region. It has been attracting mountaineers since long. It is approachable from Rishiganga side only and not from here. We were climbing a very rough terrain full of huge rocks and boulders. We had covered more than eight miles by now. We sat on a vantage point from where we got the closest and widest view of the whole mountain, which stood straight before my eyes in all its divine loftiness and splendour. It is a magnificent creation of God.

I have watched the peak from Auli-Gorson bugiyal. There, it stands amidst a cluster of peaks but here it stood all by itself like the huge majestic throne of an emperor, the Himalaya, the king of the kings, a manifestation of the lord himself. My eyes fell on a part from where a big chunk was missing. One of my companions told me that it was this part, which had Sanjeewani herb. Hanuman who was in a great hurry could not detect the herb. He pulled out the whole chunk and flew away with it to the battle field of Lanka to save the life of Laxman. There were some crimson marks on the rocks which they told me was the blood of the mountain. I took some photographs and was lost in the insatiable beauty when one member of the party said that it was now time to return as the weather was most uncertain on these heights". We came back from our memorable trekking for a late hour lunch.

We left for Joshimath the next morning with fond memories of the majestic Dronagiri and the people living in its proximity.

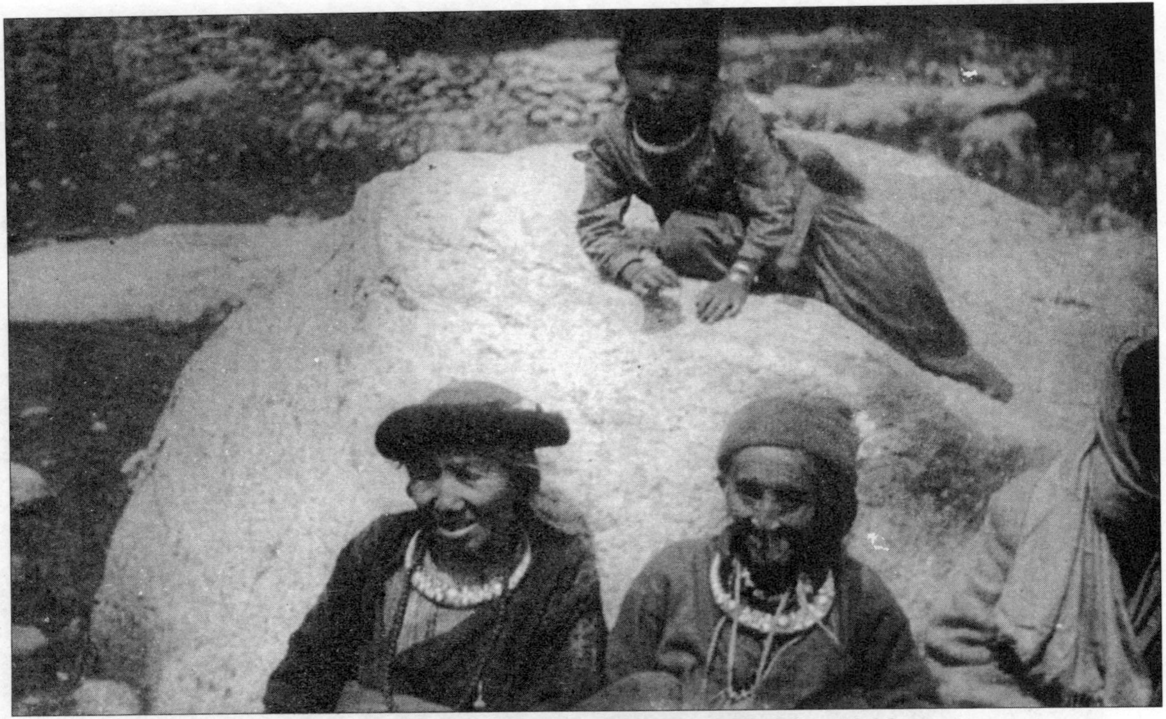

OLD HILL LADIES, BAGORI, HARSIL, 1962

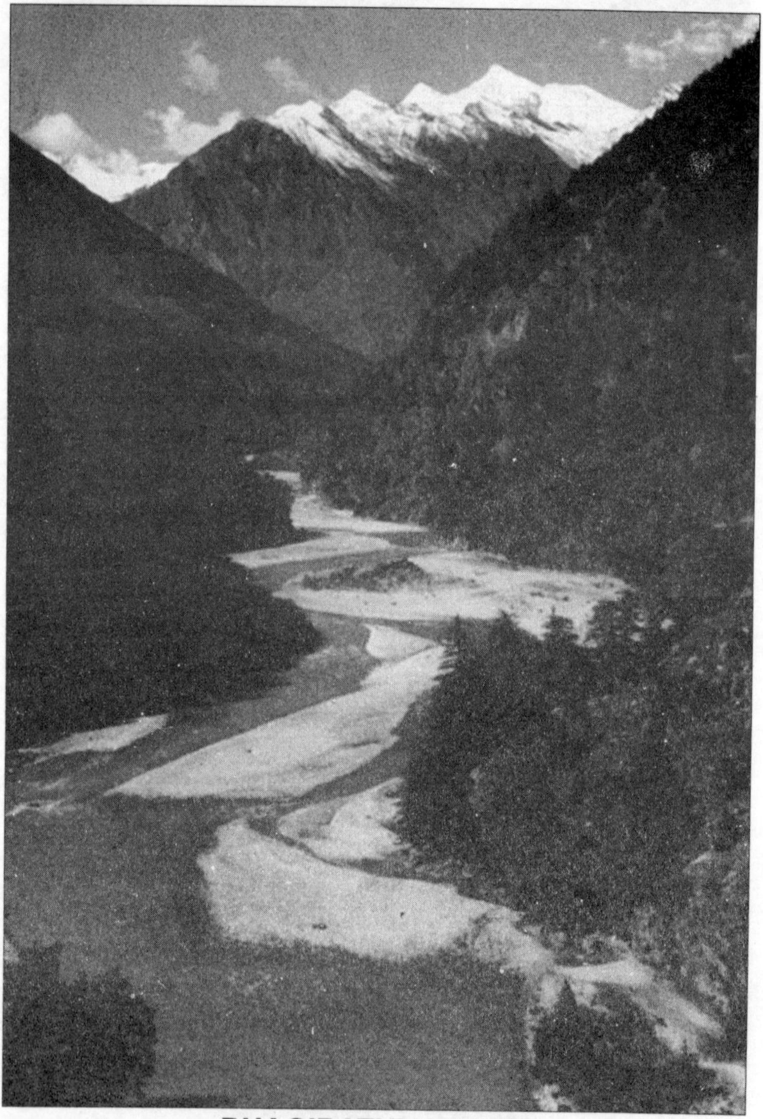

BHAGIRATHI VALLEY

21

My Days in Bhagirathi Valley

Luck smiled on me, and in September 1958 I was transferred from Joshimath to Bhatwari in Tehri district. After serving for three years in Alaknanda valley, the abode of Lord Vishnu, Mother Ganga called me to her bosom, in Bhagirathi valley, the holy place of her birth. One October evening, I reached Dharasu, 120 k. m. from Rishikesh, with my family. It was then the bus terminus on the right bank of the Bhagirathi. From here a road to the left goes to Yamunotri and the other along Bagirathi to Gangotri. Uttarkashi and Bhatwari are on this route. It is a narrow valley which widens at Matli 13 miles from Dharasu and passes through a long stretch of fertile land. It was a pleasure to walk along the paddy fields. The air was sweet with the fragrance of the ripe paddy crop ready for harvest. The golden paddy ears, rippled by the autumn breeze, were a feast to the eyes and the murmur of Bhagirathi flowing down the valley, a sweet music to the ear. As we moved to Baraethi, the next village, the scenic town of Uttarkashi, shadowed by the high mountains was in view. We reached Uttarkashi in the evening.

Uttarkashi

Nestling at the foot of Varunavat hill, in the middle of a picturesque fertile valley, extending from Asi Ganga on the North to Varuna in the South, the small town of Uttarkashi, with the villages of Gyansu and Barahat in its neighborhood, was then a Town Area. The place was also called Barahat. The holy Bhagirathi flows gently on its east making a sweeping curve to the north. Situated at an ideal altitude of 1158 meters the town is surrounded by high mountains covered by green pine and deodar forests which add to its beauty and grandeur. The celebrated temple of Baba Vishwanath (Lord Shiva) is located at a central place amid majestic deodar trees. Close by is the temple of goddess Durga with a twelve feet long copper *trisule* (trident) fixed to the ground. The trisule is said to have been erected by King Aneka Malla in the twelfth century. According to Atkinson Uttarkashi was the seat of an old dynasty. The inscription on the trisule, he says, show that it was a place of importance in the past.

Uttarkashi was then a tehsil with the court of a sub divisional magistrate. It remained the temporary head quarters of Bhatwari block from October 1955 to April 1959 because of the paucity of accommodation at Bhatwari. The divisional forest officer had his office and residence on a beautiful ridge, about a mile up, called Kot Bungalow. The valley on South East is dotted with small villages with fertile irrigated land.

It was a simple old town with houses built of mud and stones, covered with slate roofs and was known for sadhu *sanyasies* (hermits) who passed their days in spiritual pursuits in their small hermitages located near the bank of the Bhagirathi at Gyansu. Some of them lived on a ridge at Ujali. Uttarkashi grew into a big town after creation of a separate district in March 1960 and subsequently construction of the Maneri Bhali Hydro Electric Project.

Bhatwari

Love the people,
Go and live with them,
Be one of them,
Work with them,
And make them feel,
It is their achievement.

Bhatwari is 18 miles from Uttarkashi on the Gangotri route. A small village with a junior high school, dispensary and a post office, it developed into a small town after the shifting of the block head quarters in April 1959 and opening of the tehsil and the office of the Executive Engineer P. W. D. in March1960. It was connected by motor road in 1961. There is an ancient Shiva temple on a spur overlooking Bhagirathi. My residence was about 300 meters from the Ganga. I often watched her speeding down the slopes, splashing and spraying its water on the side rocks. Her sweet music would constantly vibrate in my ears.

The block had completed three years of its working when I joined in October 1958. M. P. Gairola, my predecessor, had given a good start to the development programmes and left the field machinery in perfect gear.

The block has an extensive area extending from Uttarkashi in the south to villages Nelang and Jadung 107 k. m. from Uttarkashi, on the extreme North West border, at an altitude of 10,000ft above sea level. There are a number of villages scattered along both sides of Bhagirathi and in distant pockets of the river, Pilangana and Asiganga surrounded by dense forests. The valley of river Indrawati on the East of Uttarkashi is the most fertile area in the block and has a number of villages.

The early years of Community Development were different. The country was just free from the shackles of a foreign rule. Rural areas, neglected during the long British rule, faced several problems and needed priority in their development. The Panchayat Raj Act was passed and panchayats were formed in all the villages. Members of the panchayats were elected by the raising hands in the meeting of the gram sabha. Election, however, rarely took place and impartial, unselfish and respected persons were requested and unanimously elected as Pradhan and members of the executive to shoulder the responsibility. Things are different to day and elections of gram sabhas are elaborate like assembly or parliament elections.

It was a great pleasure to work among simple and sincere people living in remote corners, untouched by the modern world. They lived the old life of their forefathers. Their culture and traditions were fashioned by the distinct topography and climate of the region they lived and were passed on from generation to generation.

I was lucky to have an excellent staff who worked in perfect team spirit. There was M. S. Rawat an experienced junior engineer who guided the gram sabhas in the design and construction of several school buildings, community centers, drinking water projects, roads and bridges. He got two major bridges constructed over the Bhgirathi at Siror and Lata to connect the villages on the left bank. The Siror Bridge was inaugurated by C. B. Gupta, chief minister U. P. who visited Bhatwari in June 1961. I introduced Rawat to him and told the Chief Minister that he was the official who designed and supervised the construction of the bridge.

"Did you take any guidance from the P. W. D?" Chief Minister enquired.

"No sir", Rawat replied.

The chief minister asked the superintendent engineer P. W. D. who was accompanying him if the bridge was correctly designed and safe.

"In fact sir, our junior engineers come to see this bridge and take hints from Rawat", The S. E. politely replied. The Chief Minister patted Rawat's back and praised him for the work.

The Chief Minister drove straight to Bhatwari and addressed a public meeting. The members of the Block Advisory Committee presented a memorandum requesting funds for some projects and sanction of a government high school at Bhatwari.

Opening of a high school in those days was more difficult than of a degree collage today. I was pursuing the proposal with the Education Department and pressing the demand in the zonal meetings for last two years. I put the request to some ministers who visited Bhatwari in 1960 but there was no positive response.

In his speech the chief minister praised the people for the interest they were taking in development works and gave his approval to the projects proposed. For opening a government high school he said, "I appreciate your demand and interest you are taking in education. The government policy, however, is to encourage private schools. Let the public come forward and start the high school. The government will give maxim aid"

This dampened my hopes. I went to Ram Chandra Uniyal M. L. A. who was presiding the meeting and whispered in his ear. "Tell the chief minister the public here is not in a position to establish and run a high school. Please request for a government high school".

"The C. M. has concluded his speech and it is not fair to raise the point", Uniyal whispered back.

I accompanied the C. M. to community center where lunch was arranged by the members of Block Committee." You were gracious to sanction our demands for which we are grateful", I submitted and continued. "Opening of a high school by public in this remote area bordering Tibet is not possible. We are not so equipped and advanced as public down in the plains. It will take time to reach that stage. We have still to create awareness in villages to send children to school. The other border blocks have long been provided government high schools".

"These facts were not put before me by any officer". C. M. said, He looked back and called Chaturvedi his P. A. 'Note down Chaturvedi, a government order is to be issued sanctioning a government high school at Bhatwari immediately this session.".

"Are you happy now". The C. M. turned to me with a smile.

"More than that", I replied and thanked the C. M.

I informed the district magistrate. "May I announce this good news to the gathering here". I asked. "Yes" the D. M. replied.

"I feel great pleasure to say that honorable C. B. Gupta Chief Minister has just given his sanction for a government high school at Bhatwari. We are grateful to him and I thank honorable Chief Minister on your behalf." There was clapping

"You want to be doubly sure". The C. M. said with a smile.

C. B. Gupta was a very generous man. While leaving the district he said, "Your demands were far les than what I had come to offer".

All the sanctions were received within a month. There was a great problem to get land for the high school but some how it was solved. It is an intermediate college today.

As for my other staff M. D. Nautiyal was another staff member who had his own ingenious way of organizing meetings, kisan melas, the Magh Mela at Uttarkashi and the ten days Ramlila at Bhatwari. B. C. Dimari a smart official enthused life to the cooperative societies and managed the V. I. P. visits and programmes of other inspecting officers efficiently. He joined the army and retired as major. M. D. Kandapal a devoted worker of agriculture and horticulture had a charming style of persuading the villagers to adopt the improved methods of cultivation. Miss Vinod Bartwal, the Assistant Development Officer for women, organized the *mahila mangal dals* (women clubs) in villages, conducted women training camps and persuaded women to adopt improved methods of cultivation, grow vegetables and fruits. She later joined the S. S. B. a Para military organization, put up good performance and retired as area organizer. Ram Dayal Singh, village level worker, a resident of an eastern district of U. P. acclimatized himself to the cold climate of Harsil 8,000ft above sea level, learnt the local dialect and excelled in the plantation of apple and other fruit trees in villages Sukhi, Jhala, Jaspur, Bagori,Mukhwa and Dharali in the Harsil valley. In short, each worker in the field or office contributed his best.

Usha Pati Bhatt, the first District Magistrate of Uttarkashi, gave top priority to development work. He even oriented the revenue staff for this work. Deeply interested in the welfare of hills, he made comprehensive plans for the over all development of the district. Many plans were drawn out in the quietude of forest rest house at Harsil, where he loved to stay. He planned in advance the construction of junior high school buildings proposed in the five year plan. The schools, when opened had not to wait for a proper building. One of his dream projects was to turn the whole Harsil valley into a big apple growing area. The climate and the physical geography of the valley was conducive for apple and the orchard planted by Wilson decades back and some orchards in Mukhwa and Dharali villages were living examples to show the potential of the valley.

"Let us survey the whole area and collect data of annual grain produced in each holding", he told me. "We will request the government to grant that much of grain annually to the farmers if they plant apple trees on their land instead of growing grain. This subsidy will continue till the fruit crop gives the farmer better return than the production of food grains. The government will arrange proper marketing of the produce. The valley is being connected by motor road hence there will be no problem for transport. This will bring prosperity to the poor farmers". He was quite optimistic about his plan. "The plan will cost much less then the cost of constructing one kilo meter road", he said, " and if per chance the scheme is a failure, we will console ourselves that a kilo meter of road was washed away in the heavy rains".

I tried to persuade the villagers but their conservative mind was not prepared to accept the scheme. They were not prepared to stop growing food crops and shift to horticulture. We, however, were able to persuade them to plant fruit trees near their houses and on land they could spare for apple trees.

Years after my retirement I was talking to a fruit contractor, who had purchased the litchi crop of my small garden at Dehradun and asked him his next plan.

"I have to rush to Harsil to bid for the apple crop in Sukhi, Jhala and Harsil", he said.

"Is that area producing that much to attract you from here?" I asked.

"Yes, there are a number of apple orchards in Harsil area and the owners are making good money for the last several years". he replied.

I was overjoyed with the news. The dream project of Mr. Bhatt, was partially fulfilled. His main emphasis was on horticulture, sheep breeding and expansion of education in the district. It was a great pleasure to work under his guidance.

The villagers, as mentioned earlier, were simple, cooperative and genuinely interested in development work. There was Ghanshyam Singh Bhandari popularly known as *Takno*r Gandhi (Taknor is the name of the region). A fair, tall, sober, elegant and respected person, he presided over the meetings of the Block Advisory Committee. He took great interest in the collection and marketing of precious herbs which grow abundantly in the *bugiyals*"(the alpine meadows) Nain Singh sarpanch of Gorsali lead the folk dance party, particularly the Ranso dance. (a group dance lead by a leader with *chawar* "a bushy tail of Tibaten chawar cow". Ganga Singh pradhan of Bhankoli was an excellent folk dancer and lead the folk dance party of his village on the occasion of republic day celebration at Delhi; They were elated by meeting the President and the Prime Minister of India. Others whose names I would like to mention were, Surat Singh of Kuroli, Debi Singh Nismor, Mahadev Prasad and Brindra Prasad of Mukhwa, Nain

Singh of Shyaba and Shri Pati of Bhela Tipri village. There are several other names worth mentioning but it would make a long list.

Those were the days when each village tried to out do others in the race for development work. There was a tempo, a spirit to work. Each village had its drinking water project; Villages without primary school were provided new schools and a school building. The old dilapidated school buildings were replaced with new. Junior high school Bhatwari was upgraded into high school. Four junior high schools were opened at Manari, Sald, Kaldayni and Musticsaur and their buildings were constructed by the block. The village paths were improved and bridges and culverts were constructed where needed. In agriculture and horticulture sector, new improved seeds were introduced and fruit plantation was carried out on a large scale. Under animal husbandry stock man centers with dispensary, and bull center buildings were established in Saura, Sald and Musticsaur. Under the cultural development programme folk song and folk dance competitions were organized in central places. Special programmes were held on the occasion of Magh Mela and Kisan Mela and prizes were distributed to the best performers. This encouraged the rural people to revive their rich culture and folk lore. I did not know how the years passed.

22

A Tale of Two Villages

Those six years were the most memorable years of my service career. I had gained love and respect from the people and the staff and there was a deep contentment within me. Just when you think that nothing in the world can go wrong, events develop that make you realize how slender the thread of life is; rescindable at any time. As my tenure drew to a close I lost my wife. I was left shattered as I tried to cope with this tragedy.

Looking back, the sweet memory of days spent with the people and members of my staff still stirs my heart while the memory of my loving wife pierces my heart with grief.

We have our share of happiness and misery in life. It depends how ably you steer your way. My mind is full of sweet and bitter memories. Out of all these the tale of two villages is an interesting reminiscence.

In his struggle of life, man has explored and made habitable many inaccessible regions in Himalayas. The picturesque Pilangna Valley, far to the South East of Bhatwari, is one such region. It is covered with dense green forests, with wild animals like bears, pigs, barking deer, wild mountain goats etc. The alpine meadows are the habitats of the beautiful Munal birds, a majestic winged pheasant with splendid bright coloured plumage. The specious valley has three villages, Silla, Jarao and Pilang, in its lap. These villages are located between 5,000ft to 6,000 ft above sea level. The torrential Pilangna roars down the valley from her source in the snow covered Khatling glacier and meets the Bhagirathi at Malla two miles down from Bhatwari.

All the three villages are separated by dense forests. Silla is 10km from Bhatwari, on the South East, across the Bhagirathi on a hill. Jarao is 3km from Silla and Pilang is the last village some 5km from Jarao. You have to cross Pilangna River and climb 2km to reach the village. The story relates to two villages Pillang and Silla.

The primary and junior high schools in rural areas were then managed and run by the district board. The state government sanctioned a model government primary school for a village in a remote area, in each border block. The name of village Pilang was recommended and approved by the government. The school building was to be constructed by the Public Works Department. The Executive Engineer P. W. D. Bhatwari requested me to arrange the land which was to be donated by the villagers. I deputed an Assistant Development Officer and the Village Level Worker of the circle for the task. They reached the village and requested the villagers to arrange land for the school. The villagers flared up. "We don't want a school", they said. They would not listen to a word about the school and drove the officials away. They came back and related their sad experience. "It is not possible to persuade the villagers to donate the land", they said. Their account depressed me but I brushed the thought aside. I have a fascination for people living in remote villages and had some understanding of their mindset. I instructed the Village Level Worker to visit the village after a week, organize the youths and interested elders to form a bhajan mandali (a club to sing prayers or psalmodies). I asked him to take a set of musical instruments from the store for the club, stay in the village for some nights and participate in their programme. I cautioned him not to talk about the school and planned to visit the village after a couple of weeks.

The V. L. W., an experienced worker, organized the youth club which started meeting every evening. The harmonium was a prize possession and every one tried his fingers on its keys.

I went to the village after a fortnight. The V. L. W was informed in advance to arrange for musical programme in the night. The Pradhan (headman) who lived in a neighboring village requested me to stay with him and visit the village the next morning. He was bit apprehensive but I insisted for spending the night with the villagers in Pilang. We reached the village in the evening. The villagers welcomed us and made arrangement for my stay, and the programme in a specious room. It was mid winter and very cold outside.

I met the village elders, enquired about their welfare, the yield of the autumn harvest and prospects of the winter crop. "Every thing is well", they said. They had a good crop of millets, pulses and paddy due to good rains. The wheat and barley crops were progressing well. There was a talk about weather, their cattle etc but not a word about the school.

After an early dinner the villagers assembled in the room and the programme was started with a prayer. I was playing on the harmonium. I requested the young men to come forward and give their songs. At first they hesitated but on my insistence they came one after the other. They sang in chorus but would do a solo at times. They sang some touching songs, reminiscences of past events which appealed to the heart. The over crowded room became stuffy and most of them who were singing in full voice were sweating. We did not know how the time passed. It was past midnight when the programme ended. Everyone parted with a smile on his face.

The morning was bright. I got ready to take a round of the village. There was a spring in the corner of the village. Some young ladies had come to clean utensils, wash clothes and fill their pitchers. The spring is usually the exclusive resort of women where they have freedom to gossip. Small houses with slate roofs stood in rows on the slope of the hill. Young boys and girls were driving their cattle and sheep through narrow lanes to the grazing grounds and some women were cleaning the cowsheds. Winter is the lean time for agriculture. The farmers were smoking in their courtyards and as I went closer they stood up and accompanied me. At the end of the row a prominent elder of the village saw me and spread a large mat on his threshing floor. He brought a small carpet and requested me to take my seat. All the villagers sat beside me. The previous night's assembly had brought us close. They appeared to have found a close friend.

"How was last night like?" I asked.

"Extremely fine", one of them said. "Since you sent the set of musical instruments we daily sit together to sing and dance".

"Do you perform folk dance?"

"Yes we dance on festivals, during the worship of our village deity and other auspicious occasions. We have special dresses which include a long black woolen coat, black trousers, a white cotton turban and a long girdle round the waist".

"We hold folk dance shows in the Kisan Mela at Barwari and Magh Mela at Uttarkashi"; I said" I will invite you to both the places, I hope you will participate".

"Surely", they confirmed.

"You must have problems in the village", I asked.

"The great problem is of wild beasts. The bears and pigs damage our crops. We do not have a single gun to scare and drive them away".

"Why not fence the whole area? I know some villages that have done it".

"Our village has a large unwieldy area, yet it is a good suggestion and we will think over it".

Our talks were frank and the atmosphere homely. I thought the time was ripe to open my cards.

"Many of you must be interested in reading and writing", I said informally. There was a strange look on some faces.

"What do we need it for?" one of them retorted. "We are good without that".

"It does make a difference", I said. "The world is changing. Where ever I go I find villagers taking interest in schools. Most of the villages have their own school. The Bhatwari junior high school has become a high school and

Uttarkashi has still a bigger school where boys from lower schools go to study".

"And who is going to tend the cattle, take our flock of sheep for grazing, and look after the little ones at home when their mothers go out to the field?, a villager questioned.

It was a problem to convince them. In their present social and economic structure each hand was needed to shoulder the family burden. Education to them was neither a social status nor did it have any economic utility. With their hard labour, they had made themselves self sufficient. They met their meager necessities from their own resources and efforts in the village itself. They seldom moved out except to some town once a year to get salt, jaggery cloth etc. Education was not their felt need. They needed to be made aware of the ills of illiteracy and ignorance.

"Look here", I said." I belong to a village like yours except that we had a school in our village from a long past where my father and others studied. I also studied in the same school and went out for higher studies. Education helped me to find this job and I am here with you to tell you what I gained. You are now getting that gift which we got long back. It will take time for you to reap the harvest which people near Bhatwari and Uttarkashi are getting today. Their boys are in good jobs in the newly created district, and are earning money and living a better life. Here you work from morning to night and just get a square meal. Your method of cultivation is still old. You can learn better ways of farming; grow crops like fruits and vegetables which can bring you more money. You should learn to improve the breed of your sheep and get better quality and quantity of wool. Education is a must to learn all this and lead a better spiritual and material life. Our scriptures say, "A person without education, music and art is like an animal without a tail and two horns. "

My words were appealing but some die hard ones were still unimpressed. One of them stood up and said.

"Since you are insistent we will donate that spot". He pointed out a rocky mound at a distance.

"That is hardly a place for a school", I said. "Your children will tumble down the rocks".

"This situation will not arise as there will be no child in the school", He said with a smile.

I was now a bit serious and changed my tone.

"You are lucky that a government school has been sanctioned for your village. The government is constructing your building where as in other villages the villagers have to build the school building themselves. If you refuse to donate land I will get the school shifted to some other village that needs it more. The people of Silla village have been pressing me to get them a school. I will request the education department to shift this school there. They have already arranged the land. You will not get a school for long time. Remember, your children and the coming generation will curse you. They will never excuse you for this".

The arrow hit the mark. The person who had requested me to sit there stood up. He had not spoken a word so far and was just listening to the discussion.

"Do not listen to those who oppose the school", he looked at me and said. "We do need a school and will not let this chance go. I will arrange the land. Please do construct a school" He offered tea to all assembled there. He was a respected man in the village and every one seemed to follow his word. He took me to a nice plot and donated it to the school. They appeared to have felt the need and importance of a school. Every one was happy.

With the mission fulfilled, I happily returned to my head quarters.

I wrote to the Executive Engineer P. W. D. to send his official to take over the land and start construction. I next met Saklani, the District Inspector of Schools, told him the whole story and requested him to post a teacher of my choice. i suggested the name of Raghunath Prasad, (I hope I remember the name correctly), whom I knew as one of the best teachers. He will give a good shape not only to the school but to the village I told him. Saklani agreed and sent Raghunath the posting order.

I visited the village after a month. The villagers had given a spacious house to the teacher for his residence and the school had some twenty boys and girls, neatly dressed,learning the first letters. The teacher had brought with him his battery radio set which was a great attraction to the whole village. Raghunath had brought a real change in the life of the village. The villagers were happy to get a school and a good teacher.

" It is all your own achievement", I told them

"You may say so", one of them replied with a smiling face.

Two Horns and a Tail

Silla was now the only village left in the block without a school. The nearest school was two miles away and the path passed through a dense forest. The parents were afraid of the wild animals which prowled in broad day light. The villagers did not send their children to that school. I stated this fact to th D. I. O. S. "district inspector of schools" and requested him to open a school in village Silla.

"You have grabbed the maximum number of schools out of the district quota and It is now the turn of other blocks". The D. I. O. S. replied to my persistent demand.

I went to the village one day and met Ramkrishna an educated resident of the village who was constantly pressing me for the school.

"I have tried my best but the D. I. O. S has kept the proposal in the waiting list". I advised him to meet the District Magistrate, and tell him that a proposal was sent to the D. I. O. S long back by the Block Development Officer to open a school in their village Silla but he is not giving his approval. I quoted the same Sanskrit verse I had quoted to Pilang people that without education a man is like an animal without horns and a tail. I drafted an application on behalf of the village, got it signed by the villagers and gave it to Ramkrishna to present it to the D. M.

Ramkrishna sought an audience with the D. M.

'What have you come for?", the D. M. questioned.

Ramkrishna presented the application and requested with folded hands. "We do not have a school in our village Sir. Our B. D. O. has sent the proposal to D. I. O. S. long back. He has been persistently pressing for it but the D. I. O. S is not giving his approval. Our children have been deprived of their right. I have heard that a man without education is like an animal without horns and a tail. He took out two horns and a tail of a sheep from his bag and kept them on the table.

"What is this?", the D. M enquired.

I am illiterate sir", Ramkrishna said. "Please fix them to my forehead and back and I will be a complete animal then".

The D. M. smiled at him. "Pick them up!" he ordered. "You deserve to have a school; I appreciate your genuine interest and will consider your demand. You can go".

The D. M. called me the next day. "A funny man came to meet me from village Silla the other day with two horns and a tail and requested me to fix them to his body. You must have tutored him, it cannot be his brainwork".

"It is news to me sir. I did go to his village and had advised him to meet you and plead for the school but the horns and the tail part is his own ingenuity". The D. M. sent instruction to the D, I. O. S. to open a school in the village. The school started functioning and a nice school building was constructed by the villagers with monetary help from the block budget.

Thus ends the tail of the two villages.

23

Bhatwari to Harsil

Bhagirathi valley excels in beauty and grandeur. Its fertile land, high mountains, glittering snow peaks, dense forests and lush meadows made it an abode of the sages, saints and hermits in the hoary past. They spent their days in contemplation of god and attained inner happiness and bliss in the tranquil hills and dales. The valley now attracts thousands of pilgrims, tourists and mountaineers each year. Consecrated by the holy Ganga, its sacred vibrations sanctify all those who come to her with faith and humble heart.

I had left the readers at Bhatwari. I resume the march to the holy shrine of Gangotri and Gaumukh the source of Bhagirathi.

It used to be a pleasure to walk on a well maintained road with fellow pilgrims coming from different parts of the country. Walking is the way to explore and absorb the beauty of nature. If you are interested, you will find so many things on the way. You see the cultivated fields with rich crops, cattle grazing on green grasslands, high mountains, dense forests, the snow peaks, and beautiful birds of different species. By your side is the Holy River gurgling, changing shape and form speeding down the rocks and at places flowing down placidly. Nine miles from Bhatwari, Gagnani which is known for its hot water spring, was a nice halting place. There was a small market, a Kali Kamali dharmshala on the right bank and a forest rest house on a spur, near the hot water spring on the left. The market, the dharmshala and a long stretch of the road on the right bank were swept away in a flash flood in 1978. The motor road was aligned on the left bank. The road passes through a steep hill eroded by the construction of the motor road. A grim tragedy took place in 1980 when a party of ten people coming back from Harsil got buried beneath the debris which rolled down the hill just as they were crossing a loose portion. There is a bridge over the river at Dabrani and then a climb up to Sukhi.

Sukhi

Perched on a beautiful hill Sukhi is a small village 2744 M above sea level. The village which grew millets and potatoes in the past is now proud of its apple trees. I have often stayed here during my tours and had a delightful time watching the lofty mountain on the East covered with rich deodar forest and glittering snow peaks. It was thrilling to find the uproarious Bhagirathi cascading down in white foam through the steep rocky hill.

An easy climb of three km takes you to Sukhi top which presents a panoramic view of the picturesque Harsil valley. On the left are some rugged hills with scanty vegetation. The other side is lush green with deodar forests. It is a plain valley 24km long up to Janglala. With Bhagirathi, meandering slowly on a smooth sandy bed, wooded mountains on both sides and white snow peaks far on the northeast, the serene valley looks like a fairy land.

Jhala

From Sukhi top the road descends down to Jhala. The bridle path in those days passed through the right bank to Harsil. The motor road now crosses Bhagirathi below Jhala, turns to the left and runs parallel to the river up to Jangla. Jhala is the biggest village of the area and has now a number of apple orchards. Across the river is the community orchard of the village planted by the efforts of late, Nag Dutt, pradhan of the gram sabha, in the year 1958. I am told that the orchard is giving good yield of apples and is an asset to the gram sabha. It is a rare example, for most of the community orchards have been a failure. I remember, after the China war in October 1962, I went there in December to organize defense society. An early snow fall had covered the whole area with thick snow. I stayed in the village for three days. The village contributed generously to the national defense fund. The ladies came forward and took out their silver ornaments like silver necklace, bangles etc and donated them to the National Defense Fund.

Harsil

Nestled among majestic deodar trees, at. an altitude of 2620 meters above sea level, Harsil is an enchanting sylvan retreat in the idyllic Bhagirathi valley. The bubbling sound of the sparkling Jalandari and Kakora rivers, speeding down from both sides of a high mountain on its west and the murmur of the Bhagirathi meandering through the meadows on the east, add music to its scenic beauty.

On a clear day in July 1959 I reached here with Mr S. P. Watel assistant development commissioner border area.

"What a charming place sir?" I said, as we sat down in the balcony of the forest rest house which was once the residence of the famous Wilson.

"Yes, as beautiful as Kashmir valley", said watel who belonged to Kashmir.

Wilsons grand mansion and the beautiful apple orchard planted by him impressed me and I was interested to know about the great man.

The picturesque Harsil, once on the pilgrim route, has now been bypassed by the motor road which runs on the opposite hill on the left bank of the Bhagirathi. The buses drive straight to Gangotri and the pilgrims can only enjoy the beauty of the place if they break their journey here.

24

The Legendary Wilson

During the second half of nineteenth Century the names Harsil and WIilson were synonymous. It was Wilson's Harsil or Harsil's Wilson. Long years have imperceptibly erased his name from public memory and pushed it into the dark vaults of the past. People know little about Wilson, the legendry man of Harsil.

Frederick E. Wilson, a young deserter from the British army, a lonely English man, trekked into this remote corner of Tehri State some years after the Afgan war of 1842. He found shelter in Mukhwa, a village of the priests of Gangotri temple, 3km from Harsil. A harijan family was kind to offer him a room in their small house. The village women were afraid of the tall sturdy white man, the kind they had never seen before. He mixed with the local people helped them in their field and domestic work and nursed the sick. He picked up their dialect and became one of them.

During my visit to Mukhwa village in 1959 I met Massy, an aged person, son of Wilson's brother-in-law Subdhanu. Massy lived in a nice building built by Wilson for his in-laws. I enquired from him the details about Wilson's life.

"I do not remember to have seen him", he said. He, however, gave me many facts about Wilson's life, his adventures and his big timber business which he had heard from his father and other relations. He gave me an old diary, maintained by his late father, written in English. It related to the period after Wilson's death and contained copies of his letters to Wilson's wife Raimata and son Charley Wilson. They were requests for financial help from time to time and about his visits to Charley Wilson's house at Mussoorie where he was nicely treated. The diary was lost while shifting the luggage on transfer.

To earn his living, Wilson, an excellent hunter, started hunting musk deer, fur animals and monals, a majestic pheasant with remarkable plumage like that of a pea cock. He distributed the meat of his kill to villagers, won their love and regard and minted big money by selling musk, a rare and costly substance found in a special gland in the male musk deer. Musk has a great demand for manufacturing medicines and perfumes. The Himalayan furs and the bright monal feather, a novelty and luxury to English ladies, added gold to his coffer. The Government has now totally banned the killing of these rare animals and birds. The offence is punishable with a fine and imprisonment.

His sharp eagle eyes next fell on the rich virgin deodar forests of the area. He approached the Maharaja Tehri and got his permission to cut and exploit the dense forests on nominal lease. He employed hundreds of men and for years, his unrivaled and unbridled axe, continued felling tall deodar trees which were sawed into logs, hauled to the river and floated down to Hardwar by the swift current of the Ganga. He was the pioneer who innovated this novel method of transporting timber by water channels and rivers. It was followed by successive forest contractors after him.

A man of acumen and business foresight he made a fortune by selling timber to the Railways which were spreading their net throughout the country during the hey days of the British Raj.

Wilson fell in love with his landlord's sister and married her. He purchased a large tract of land in Harsil between river Jalandari and Kakora Gad and built a majestic mansion with a big store house in the back yard. He planted apple orchards on spacious plots on both sides of his house. The local people told me that he brought the choicest varieties of apple plants from England. The apples of his orchard became famous for their bright colour, aroma, juice and taste. Wilson encouraged the farmers of neighboring villages to plant orchards and distributed plants free of cost. Progressive farmers of Mukhwa and Dharali took inspiration and planted a good number of trees. Dasharath Prasad of Mukhwa and Man Pati of Dharali had flourishing apple gardens when I was there. A special variety of apple developed by Dashrath Prasad was named Dashrath apple by the horticulture department. Wilson also introduced rajma,(a Variety of bean) potatoes and wheat in the area.

After the death of his wife, Wilson married her niece Raimata, a beautiful young lady and had three sons. He expanded his timber business and became a very wealthy man and the owner of large property. He constructed houses at Mussoorie and Dehradun. His son Charley Wilson was the proprietor of the famous Charl Ville hotel at Mussoorie. This spacious building now houses the prestigious I. A. S. Acadmy. His other two sons died young. Wilson maintained the long bridal path from Mussoorie to Harsil and constructed bridges where necessary. There were no motor roads then. He had his own rest houses en route between Mussoorie and Harsil at Jhalki, Dhanaulti, Kanatal Bhaldiyana, Dharasu, Nakuri, Uttarkashi, Maneri and Gagnani. After years of a life, full of adventures, Frederick. E. Wilson, the man who had come for hiding in the remote Bhagirathi valley with just a gun, died a millionaire. He was buried in a grave yard at Mussoorie

Wilson was survived by his eldest son Charley Wilson who married an English girl. He lived for some years at Mussoorie and left for England where he settled with his family. Wilson's property was taken over by the forest department of Tehri State. All his rest houses including his bungalow at Harsil were turned into forest rest houses. I have spent several nights in his big Mansion at Harsil during my tour of that area. Some say that he still comes galloping his horse on some full moon nights and the sound of his boots echo within the rest house but I never heard the sound though at times I was the sole occupant of the huge house.

I could not get the year Wilson died but was told that he died at quite an old age. With his death the mirth and gaiety of Harsil went away. The grand mansion which had seen his rise to the sky became desolate. A strange silence engulfed the whole valley which once resounded with the clatter of his horses and the noise of his labour force which constantly moved up and down the valley pushing the deodar logs back to the main stream, and doing several other duties.

Wilson is said to have plundered and ruined the rich forests but S. P. Sahi who was D. F. O. Uttarkashi during 1962-64 thought otherwise. I often met him when he came to Bhatwari and talked about Wilson. In Sahi's opinion Wilson was a good forester who removed the dead wood, culled the trees which had outlived their age and were an obstruction to the new growth. He rejuvenated the century old forests. Sahi searched out the old photographs of Wilson and his wife Raimata, got them developed and framed in a bigger size and put them on the walls of Harsil, Bhatwari and Dharasu rest houses.

A century has passed; some old men of the area still remember Wilson or Hul Singh as he was popularly called by local people. His bungalow, which was once the coveted place for the visitors to stay is said to be in bad shape now. New rest houses have come up for the visitors to stay. I wish the century old Wilson house could be maintained as a heritage from the past.

Wilson was the man who brought Harsil on the tourist map. He made the hill journey comfortable by erecting rest houses at suitable distances on the pilgrim route. He practically demonstrated what the rich fertile valley can yield. He will be remembered for the sweet, juicy apples and the tasty beans. He was a pioneer horticulturist, a man of the soil.

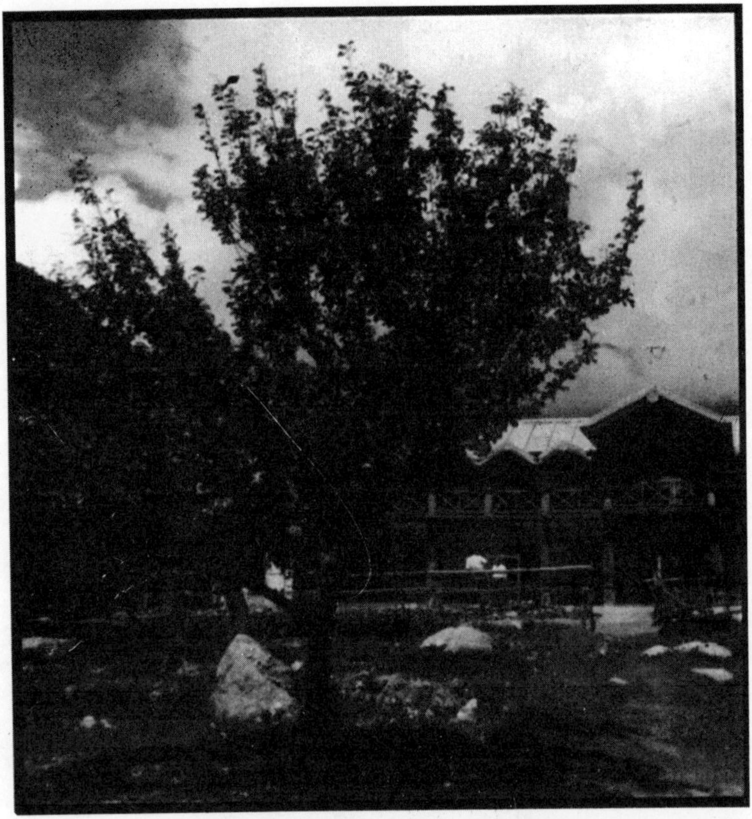

WILSON HOUSE HARSIL

25

The Legends of Ganga

"Among mountains, I am the Himalayas and among rivers, I am Janhavi, (the Ganga)"! So says Krishna to Arjuna in a concise declaration of his *Vibhuties-*, his endless glorious manifestations (Gita ch 10). This is the highest compliment given by the Lord to the Himalaya and his loving daughter Ganga. Ganga reflects the divinity and purity of the Brahman. She is the personification of a beautiful goddess, a manifestation of divine feminine energy, depicted in Puranas as Kali and Dugra. In Indian mythology she is called "*Sursari* ", "the river of gods".

Hindu mythology is vast, significant and interesting. The stories and events are coherent, logically connected and reflect the bright imagination, dreams and fancies of ancient poets, writers and dramatists who have woven many tales around gods and goddesses. The epics Ramayan, Mahabharata and Puranas are resplendent with the lore of Hindu gods. Kalidas, the great Sanskrit poet and dramatist of a later age has surpassed many writers in poetic fancy and flight of imagination. His poetic description of the Himalayas, the rebirth of Sati as daughter of the King of Himalaya, her growing into an exquisite beauty and the austerities she undertook to win

Shiva, in his great epic "Kumarshambhwa," is unmatched in literature. The adventure of Kamdev, the god of love shooting his flowery arrow at Shiva, followed by Shiva's anger and his reducing Kamdev to ashes is thrilling.

In popular Hindu mythology Brahma, Vishnu and Shiva are the three divine functionaries of Brahman, the supreme power. They are responsible for creation, preservation and destruction, a process which goes on ceaselessly. They are called *Tridev* (the Trinity). Brahma creates the universe out of self contemplation. Vishnu preserves the universe and ensures its continuance. He comes to earth as its savior when he finds righteousness decaying and establishes dharma, the world order. Shiva is absorbed in deep meditation with his gaze inward till the time comes for him to dissolve the universe. This eternal cosmic process called *ritam* in Vedas keeps the universe in perfect order.

There are other gods and functionaries as well. Ganesh also called, the vighneshwara removes all obstacles and overcomes challenges of life. He is the son of Shiva and Parvati and worshipped at the initiation of rituals. There is Agni the fire god, Surya the Sun god. Indra the god of rain, Varuna the god of water, Saraswati the goddess of knowledge, Laxmi the goddess of wealth, Kali the primordial mother, the power of Shiva and Ganga the divine goddess of purity, holiness and truth.

All these deities are reverently worshipped by Hindus in numerous temples along the length and breadth of India. People go to these temples with their offerings, singing devotional songs and reciting mantras for material wealth, progeny, power and prosperity. There are some who go for peace and spiritual attainment. Despite the multiplicity of gods and goddesses, there is a perfect unanimity among Hindu devotees that behind all these different gods there is one power, one supreme god called Brahman who is the real absolute power.

Ganga is one of the prominent deities of this great pantheism. She is the incarnation of Sati who herself was incarnated from Kali, the daughter of Brahma. Wedded to Shiva she became an adornment on his forehead. She is divine knowledge, truth, and purity that trickles out from Shiva's locks and flows in all the three worlds.

The Holy Ganga is the most worshipped river in the world. She is affectionately called Ganga *Mayya* (mother) by her devotees. Every inch of her course, from her source in the Himalayas to Gangasagar where she meets the sea, is holy. She gets uniform love, regard and worship throughout her long journey of 1550 miles from the source to the sea. Her touch sanctifies the waters of her numerous tributaries and most of them suffix Ganga to their name.

The water of holy Ganga is full of minerals and herbs and does not contaminate for days together. It is said that Ganga water kills cholera germs. A bath in the Ganga will wash away all the sins. One who dies near its bank is supposed to go to heaven. People bring the dead bodies of their near and dear for cremation at the cremation grounds on its bank and those living far away carry the ashes of their dead ones to immerse in the Ganga at Hardwar, Varanasi and Prayag.

On auspicious days, bathing festivals are held on its bank in many towns. The biggest festival called Kumbh Mela is held at Hardwar and Prayag Raj after every six years and it witnesses millions of devotees who throng to Har Ki Pauri at Hardwar and Sangam at Prayag Raj.

There are a number of temples dedicated to the goddess right from Gangotri where she is said to have descended from heaven in long past. The mouth of the glacier from where she comes out has receded 18 kilometers from Gangotri to Gaumukh. Another celebrated temple dedicated to the goddess is at Har Ki Pauri at Hardwar, the gateway for the Himalaya. There are a number of Shiva temples in towns along its course the most celebrated are at Prayag, Varanasi, Gaya and Gangasagar which are, visited by thousands of pilgrims round the year.

Ganga is synonymous with culture, civilization and prosperity of India which grew and flourished along its bank. Its groves were the peaceful shelter for saints and sages who spent their lives in the deep contemplation of god and took India to spiritual heights.

The fertile land between the river Yamuna and Ganga called Doab has been formed by the rich alluvial soil brought by these rivers from the high Himalayan Mountains, and has made it a very productive part of India. Known as Aryavarta, the land of Aryans, it has been the cradle of rich Aryan culture and civilization from long past and became the center of art, literature and music. It was from here that the unique culture and humanity of India spread to the whole country. Ganga is thus the heart of India and one cannot think of India without Ganga.

The Legend of Ganga According to the Bhagwat Purana

Once, Bali a mighty demon king ruled the earth. Indra the king of heaven had defeated him in the past. To avenge his defeat and add heaven to his empire Bali attacked

Indra and defeated him. Indra went into hiding. The gods and their mother Aditi prayed to Vishnu and requested him to get their kingdom restored. Vishnu promised help and took incarnation as Baman (the dwarf).

When he grew up, the dwarf god went to Bali's palace dressed as a Brahmin boy. Bali who was renowned for his charity welcomed him, washed his feet and offered a seat.

"Your visit has purified my palace", said Bali. "It will be my fortune to serve you. Please let me know your mission. I promise to give you whatever you desire",

"I just want three paces of land", said the Dwarf.

Bali was surprised with this strange demand." What will you do with such a small piece of land measured with three steps of your tiny feet? Bali said and requested the boy to ask for something large.

"Three steps of land is more than sufficient for me", confirmed the boy with a smile on his face.

Bali took water in his palm from a jug as a ritual for keeping the promise and requested the Brahmin boy to measure the land.

Lo! There was a miracle. The Dwarf stretched his body and covered the earth and the sky. In one step the god measured the whole earth and extended his second step to measure heaven.

As the lotus foot of the Lord touched the heaven the whole place was illuminated with brightness. All the gods ran to welcome the lotus foot of Vishnu. Brahma washed and worshipped Vishnu's foot with holy water from his *kamandalu* (jar of the mendicants). As the water touched the foot of the Lord it took the form of the holy Ganga which started flowing out of his toe. She is called *Vishnupada* (the river that flows from the foot of vishnu) or the *Akash Ganga* (the Milky Way that flows in Paradise).

Legend in Devi Purana

Ganga stands on a very high pedestal in the Puranas, the Ramayana, the Mahabharat and other Hindu scriptures. The Devi Purana traces her origin to Kali, the supreme manifestation of the mother goddess. It is said that Lord Shiva performed great austerities to win the love of the goddess and have her as his life partner. The goddess was pleased, agreed to take a divine form and remain his wife till eternity. Kali took birth as Daksha Prajapati's daughter and was named Sati. She grew up a sublime lady, a perfect symbol of beauty and married Shiva. After some years Daksh developed hatred for Shiva. He performed a yagya in which he invited all the gods except Shiva. He insulted him by putting his image at the entrance of the hall. Sati, Shiva's devoted wife could not bear the humiliation of her husband and ended her life at the sacrificial altar.

Shiva was greatly shocked to hear from Narad, "the universal wanderer", the sad news of Sati's death. It was a severe blow that shattered him completely. Mad with grief and anger he asked Virvadra his valiant warrior to destroy Daksha's altar of sacrifice and kill him. In a rage he ran to the altar where Sati's body was lying. He picked up the body, placed it over his head and started a terrifying dance that violently shook the earth. Gods and all the living beings got scared. "The earth will come to its untimely end if Shiva continues his mad dance;" they thought. "Sati's body will not decay till it is separated from

Shiva". They requested Vishnu to separate Sati's body and stop Shiva from his mad dance. Vishnu became invisible and started dismembering Sati's body imperceptibly into pieces with his Sudarshan Chakra. The fifty-one places where the parts of her pious body fell became the sacred places of worship of the goddess. Shiva who was engrossed in his dance was unmindful of Vishnu's silent action but when the whole body disappeared he understood Vishnu's trick. He was enraged and cursed Vishnu that he too will suffer separation from his wife in one of his incarnations.

Shiva went to the solitudes of the Himalayan peaks to lament over his great loss. Brahma and Vishnu who were grieved at Sati's death went to console Shiva and requested him to be calm. Shiva composed himself and went to Kamroop hill the holy seat of the goddess to meditate. After years of his austerities the goddess, the world mother, appeared before Shiva.

"I am pleased with your penance", the goddess said." Let me know your wish".

Shiva opened his eyes and made obeisance to the goddess. "Be thou my wife again as you had been in your previous incarnation as Sati", Shiva requested.

The goddess smiled and said, "I will soon come in my partial incarnation as Ganga daughter of king Himalaya. I will marry you in heaven. After my death you took me on your head and danced over the earth and so I will live as an adornment for your long, coiled, matted tresses. That will be my eternal abode. In my full incarnation I will come as Himalaya's second daughter and will adore the left half of your body and be your eternal mate". With this boon the goddess disappeared. Shiva was once again lost in his contemplation.

King Himalaya, Lord of the mountains ruled over the high Himalayan region. His kingdom was resplendent with jewels, gold, silver and several other precious metals. With lush green valleys, meadows and white snow peaks heaven appeared to have descended down to earth. It became the abode of mendicants, saints and sages who spent their long life in deep contemplation of god. It was here that the vedas were revealed to them and it was here that the rich Aryan culture and civilization was born, flourished and spread over the world.

King Himalaya married Maina the beautiful daughter of Sumeru king of the majestic golden mountain Sumeru. A most pious couple they were dear to their subjects. For long years they had no child. They went to the quietude of the forests and prayed to mother goddess to bless them with a daughter in her image. The goddess who had promised Shiva that she would again take a form found Maina the most suitable mother and Himalaya a perfect father. Pleased with their penance, she fulfilled their wish and took birth as their daughter on the third day of Vaisakh(corresponding to the last week of April) in the bright half of the lunar month. Maina and Himalaya were filled with boundless joy. There were jubilations all over their kingdom. The gods were equally happy and showered celestial flowers on earth. In a splendid celebration the child was named Ganga by the high priests.

A beautiful child on earth Ganga grew up like the waxing moon. One day king Himalaya was sitting in his palace with his loving daughter by his side when Narada came to him. The king stood up, welcomed and paid obeisance to him. He washed his feet and offered him a seat.

"It is my good fortune that you are here to bless us", the king said.

"I have come to see your daughter", Narad said and politely requested Ganga to come to him.

Ganga went and saluted Narad. Narada touched her feet and said," I am blessed oh king! And do you know who your daughter is?"

"I only know that she is my daughter. You are the all knower and can tell better", the king replied.

Narada smiled, looked at the king and said, your daughter is the partial incarnation of goddess Sati the consort of Lord Shiva in her former life. She has taken form to get Shiva her Lord".

There was a glow on Ganga's face as Narada uttered the name of her Lord. She lowered her eyes and went to her father.

"Brahma will come to you to beg for your daughter", Narad said. "He will take her to heaven and offer her to Shiva. I request you to accede to his request".

Narad took leave and went straight to Brahmlok. Making obeisance to Brahma he said, "Goddess Sati, my Lord, has taken birth as Ganga, king Himalaya's daughter".

"It is true and you know Narad", Brahma continued, "Shiva is displeased with all the gods especially Vishnu for dismembering Sati's body. Bereaved and broken hearted he has retired to the solitudes of the Kamroop hills and is steeped in deep meditation. Creation will come to an end if he continues his detachment and does not join the trinity. He has to share his part in this play of the universe. Call Indra and other gods. We will go to king Himalaya and request him to give us his daughter. We will bring her to heaven, invite Shiva and offer him his bride.

Here, in her father's house in the Himalayas Ganga had grown up into a splendid lady. She was full of virtues and a personification of beauty. She was always lost in the thoughts of her Lord Shiva and impatient to meet him. She knew that Brahma will soon come to beg her from her father who will be reluctant to give her as she was too dear to him. One night she came in her father's dream in her full divine form, riding her crocodile and said, "I am the primordial power the mother goddess. In my former incarnation I was Sati Shiva's consort and now Ganga your daughter. I have taken birth to be with Shiva. Brahma will come to take me. Please fulfill his request and do not grieve at my parting". After saying these words the goddess disappeared.

Brahma and Indra reached Himalaya's palace. The king received them and performed all the welcome rituals worthy of the great gods. He offered them their seats, stood with folded hands and requested them to give him an opportunity to serve them.

"Oh Lord of the mountains!", Brahma said, "you are renowned for your generosity and charity in the three worlds. We have come with a mission to beg from you your loving daughter Ganga, who is an incarnation of Sati Shiva's consort. Shiva has detached himself from the universe and meditating in the solitudes of the Kamroop hill after the death of Sati. We want to take Ganga to heaven and offer her to Shiva for the well-being of the universe. You will help us and grant our request".

Himalaya who had already been briefed in his dream by the goddess said with wet eyes, "A daughter does not stay in her father's house for long. She has to be given away in marriage to a worthy husband. It is my great fortune that she will get Shiva as her husband, who constantly remains in her heart. I will bear this unbearable parting".

Himalaya clasped his loving daughter in his arms. Ganga tried to calm him. In her sweet soft voice she said, "Father do not grieve. Allow me to go to heaven to meet my Shiva. I will be close to you and come to your lap one day".

Brahma and the gods were very happy and took goddess Ganga with them to heaven. Brahma asked Narada to go to Shiva and request him to come to heaven.

Narada hurried to the Kamroop hills, the holy seat of mother goddess, where Shiva was performing penance. He passed through a dense forest covered with the shadows of tall trees embraced by creepers. The air was cool, scented with the fragrance of white jasmine flowers. The groves were full of birds singing sweet melodies to the glories of the goddess. Narada was enchanted with the beauty of the hills and the surroundings. He moved on and from a distance saw Shiva sitting on a rock like mount absorbed in samadhi. The whole place was shining brilliantly with the radiance of a thousand sons radiating from Shiva. Narada's eyes were dazzled. A great silence, an absolute calm pervaded the atmosphere. A sudden fear seized Narada's heart. A little movement, a small noise may disturb Shiva from his self absorption and invite his wrath. He shuddered to open his mouth and convey Brahma's message. How to accomplish the mission he was sent for? He thought for a while, gathered courage and with silent steps went close to Shiva and spoke softly. "Oh ever blissful, omnipotent Lord be pleased on humble Narada who has come to you with a message from Brahma. Please withdraw yourself from deep contemplation for a moment. Sati your inseparable mate has taken incarnation as king Himalaya's daughter. He repeated the name of the goddess Sati several times. The word Sati started ringing in the air and distracted Shiva. Shiva opened his eyes, looked around and saw Narada standing with folded hands. With a smile on his face Shiva welcomed Narada and requested him to take his seat.

"Where is Sati?" he enquired.

"Sati, your loving wife",. Narada said, "Has come in her incarnations as king Himalaya's daughter Ganga. Brahma has brought her to heaven where she is impatiently waiting for you. Brahma has invited you to Brahmlok".

Shiva's face became radiant with joy. The luminous image of Sati came before his eyes. He stood up and accompanied Narada to heaven. Many of Shiva's attendants followed them.

Brahma and the gods who had assembled in heaven gave Shiva a big ovation.

Shiva was married to Ganga in a great ceremony attended by gods and sages.

It was a unique reunion. Ganga stood before Shiva, her Lord, the ocean of consciousness, who held her in his arms.

"Let me be an adornment in your unending tresses, the curly locks of your head. It will be my eternal abode now. You will be called *Gangadhar* (Lord of Ganga). In my full incarnation I will be your Uma and reside in the left half of your body. You, my Lord, will then be called *Ardhanarishvara* (half god and half goddess). I will be the glory of your head and Uma the kinetic energy of your heart. We both will partake with you in your highest vision. I was the river of heaven till now but with you the Lord of the universe I will flow in all the three worlds, the Celestial, Terrestrial and the Subterranean and will be called *Tripathga*(river of the three worlds). Lift me up my Lord," Ganga requested. Shiva lifted Ganga and she was in his tresses. The bridal couple left for Kailash, Shiva's eternal abode.

Legend from Valmiki Ramayan

Maharshi Valmiki the primal Sanskrit poet has beautifully described the origin and descent of the holy Ganga from heaven to earth in his great epic, the Ramayan.

The Puranas have divided the world time scale into four ages, The *Satyug*, (golden age) *Treyta*, (silver) *Dwapar*, (copper) and *Kalyug* the Iron Age. Righteousness, they say, goes on declining from satyug to kalyug.

During Treytayug king Dashrath was ruling the vast kingdom of Ayodhya. He was a brave, righteous and benevolent king. He had four sons, Ram, Laxman, Bharat and Satrughan. They were brave, illustrious, learned and master of archery. The eldest son Ramchandra was an incarnation of Lord Vishnu, the god who sustains the universe.

As time passed the evil forces started rising. Ravana the great demon king and his followers began oppressing the saints, sages and ascetics. Maharshi Vishwamitra, a great sage of the age, was performing a yagya (sacrifice) in his hermitage in the forest. Two demons Marich and Subaru lived in that area. They would often come and defile his alter with blood and bones. The sage went to king Dashrath and requested him to send Ram and Laxman to drive away the demons. The king was reluctant but allowed both the sons to go with Vishwamitra after Vashistha his royal priest persuaded him. Vishwamitra came to his hermitage with the two princes and lighted the alter fire. The two demons saw the fire and rushed towards it like a storm. They spilled blood over the alter and ran to attack Ram and Laxman who were guarding the sage. Ram killed Subahu with one arrow and aimed the other towards Marich who fled to the far South. Vishwamitra praised Ram for his valor, sanctified the whole place and completed the yagya.

In the mean time Vishwamitra received an invitation from Janaka, the king of Mithila, to attend a great yagya he was performing at his palace. The sage asked the two princes to accompany him to Mithila where they would see a great bow, the heaviest one in the world. No warrior on earth or god in heaven had been able to string it so far. The celestial bow was gifted by Lord Shiva to king Janaka after the completion of a great sacrifice in the past.

The princes got interested and accompanied the sage. They walked through dense forests full of wild animals and birds. On the second day they reached the bank of the holy Ganga, worshipped by sages. They camped near its bank, bathed and offered prayers and holy water to their ancestors.

Ram was enchanted by the serenity of the river. He requested the sage to tell him all about the holy river, its origin, how it flows in the three worlds and meets the ocean

There was a smile on Vishwamitra's face. "I am pleased with your inquisitiveness. This question was once asked by Narada to Lord Shiva. Let me relate the legend as told by Shiva", the sage said.

"There a great mountain in the north called Himalaya the king of mountains. Its peaks are covered with perennial snow and are full of jewels and precious metals. It is ruled by king Himalaya. The king had a daughter named Ganga incarnation of goddess Sati, Brahma requested the king to give him his daughter Ganga to marry her to Lord Siva for the well being of the gods and the universe. The king agreed and Brahma took her to heaven where she was married to Shiva and lived with him in heaven. She is called Tripathga, river of the three worlds for she flows in heaven, on the earth and in the under world. I will now relate to you the story of her descent to the earth".

"Ram, you belong to the ancient illustrious family of Ekshaku son of Manu the originator of the human race and grandson of the sun god. In this lineage there was once a great king Sagar who ruled the vast kingdom of Ayodhya. He had two wives, Keshni and Sumati. For long they had no child. Worried the king went to the hermitage of sage Bhrigu and performed penance for a long time. The sage was pleased and asked the king for a boon.

The king stood with folded hands and said. "I have no son to inherit my kingdom. Please bless my queens and fulfill my desire".

"One of your queens will have one son and the other 60,000. Let the queens express their choice". The sage said.

The elder queen Keshni wanted one son and the other 60,000.

"Be it so", the sage gave his blessing.

In course of time Keshni got one son and Sumati 60,000, sons.

Asumanjh, son of Keshni and the eldest among all the brothers grew into a cruel and troublesome man. He used to pick up children from the town and drown them in the river. The king was fed up and banished him from the kingdom. Ashmanjh had a son named Ansuman. He was brave, gentle, affectionate and dear to his grandfather.

Sagar was a religious, virtuous and godly king. Once he decided to hold an "Ashwamedh yagya". This yagya is performed to establish supremacy over all other rulers in the region. A sturdy horse is consecrated and after the completion of the yagya is set free to roam in other territories. Any king who tries to capture the horse is attacked and subdued. On its return the victorious horse is sacrificed. The great yagya began. Indra the king of heaven got jealous and scared. Sager, he thought, on completion of the yagya, will take over his kingdom. He stole the horse and hid it. This obstructed the yagya. "The yagya cannot proceed without the horse", the priests said.

The king was worried. He ordered his 60,000 sons to move out and bring the horse. The princes spread in all the directions and made a thorough search from high Himalayas in the North to the Vindhyas in the South. They finally went to the Far East and found their horse grazing near the hermitage of sage Kapila. Wild with anger the princes abused and accused the sage who was sitting deep in meditation. In great anger the sage opened his eyes. A big flame of fire flashed out and burnt all the 60,000 sons of Sagar

King Sagar got worried when his sons did not return. He asked his grandson Ansuman to search for his uncles and the horse.

Ansuman followed the path taken by his uncles. He covered a long distance and reached sage Kapila's hermitage. He had the shock of his life when he saw a great heap of ash which was the remains of his 60,000, uncles. The horse was grazing nearby. Deeply hurt, the prince searched for water to sprinkle over the ashes of the departed souls for their liberation, but there was no water anywhere. Suddenly Garur, the maternal uncle of the 60,000. Princes appeared before him.

"Your uncles", he said," have been reduced to ashes by sage Kapila's curse and a handful of ordinary water from tanks and streams will not liberate them. Only the holy Ganga, the elder daughter of king Himalaya, which flows in paradise, can liberate them if she can be brought here and she flows over the ashes. Take the horse to king Sagar to complete the yagya.

Ansuman went back with the horse and told the king about the tragic death of his uncles and the way of their liberation as revealed to him by Garur. Bereaved Sagar somehow completed the yagya.

Sagar tried his best but could not bring Ganga. After ruling for 30, 000, years he left for his heavenly abode.

Ansuman succeeded his grand father and after ruling for many years handed over his kingdom to his son Dalip. Dalip was a brave and devout king. He also made efforts to bring Ganga but could not get success. Dalip was succeeded by Bhagirath.

Bhagirath was a righteous king. He was a good ruler and worked for the welfare of his subjects, but the thought of liberating his 60,000. Ancestors always pricked his mind. He had no son and that was an additional worry. He handed over the management of his kingdom to his ministers and went to the shrine of sage Bhrigu to achieve his mission. He sat in deep meditation and after a thousand years of penance Lord Brahma appeared and said.

"I am pleased with your penance, my son. You can ask for a boon".

May the 60,000 sons of Sagar receive the holy water of mother Ganga by my hand and their souls rest in peace in heaven? I also pray to bless me with a son to continue the Ekshaku dynasty".

"Be it so", Brahma said. "I will persuade the holy Ganga to descend to earth to liberate your ancestors. There is, however a big problem. The earth will not be able to sustain the tremendous force of Ganga. It will split. But who will hold Ganga and break her force? He remembered Shiva the only god who can save the earth from this catastrophe. He is the only power to break the great force of Ganga. You go and pray to Lord Shiva",. Brahma said and disappeared.

King Bhagirath, a man of strong will and determination, practiced rigorous austerities. He balanced his body on his thumb and meditated on Shiva for one year.

Shiva, the Lord of Uma came, blessed Bhagirath and said." I will hold Ganga the loving daughter of king Himalaya on my forehead. You pray her to come down"

Bhagirath prayed earnestly for another year and holy Ganga expressed her consent.

Ram, the incarnation of god Vishnu, from whose toe Ganga had emerged in Paradise, was listening the legend narrated by sage Vishwamitra with rapt attention. Sage Vishwamitra paused for a while, looked to the sky and the holy Ganga nearby and continued. "Our mythology is full of celestial events and miracles but the descent of mother Ganga is one of the greatest celestial events and is beyond description".

The eternal, omnipotent god of the gods, Lord Shiva stood on the high Himalayan Mountain. The snow galaxy glittered with the radiance of his face. Wrapped in a tiger skin and a necklace of king cobras round his blue neck he turned his big bright eyes to the sky. Holding his mighty trident in his hand he let loose his long matted tresses which spread out in all the directions, covering the limitless space. The gods descended to earth and offered prayers. There was a big flash. Amid thunder and lightning goddess Ganga, riding her crocodile, descended from the infinite, waving her long glossy hair. The diamond crown of her head and the pearl necklace on her neck were shining brightly due to the radiance of her divine face. White foam spraying out from her torrents enveloped the sky as she rolled down with the roar of a tornado.

Shiva saw his consort, his own *Shakti* (power) dashing down in all her fury. A direct confrontation between Shakti and Shaktiman (power and the lord of power) was inevitable. The earth shivered with fear. The impregnable torrents may sweep Shiva, she thought and inundate and split her. The gods stood in prayer and implored the goddess to calm down and save the earth. Vishnu the Lord sustainer of the universe alerted *Seshnag* (the residual energy that holds the universe) to tighten its grip. There was panic everywhere.

As she came near Shiva, Ganga bowed. "Forgive me my Lord", she said. It is long since I was away. I am impatient to meet you and she dropped like a garland of lotus flowers on Shiva's forehead and merged with her Lord. Shakti was now one with Shaktiman. The cosmic law was upheld. Ganga, they say, roamed within the web of Shiva's long tresses, his matted locks and could not find a way out.

The sudden disappearance of Ganga in Shiva's locks disheartened Bhagirath but he did not accept defeat. Once again he sat in meditation and prayed to Shiva to release the mother from his locks. The benevolent Shiva allowed Ganga to trickle down to Bindu Sarover (lake) from where her waters flowed in seven streams to different directions. Whadini, Pavani and Nalini flowed to the East, Suchakshna, Sita and Sindhu to the West. The seventh stream Bhgirathi Ganga followed Bhagirath who was riding his divine chariot. The legend of celestial Ganga, her journey from heaven to earth, is unique and matchless in the annals of Indian mythology

Rippling through glaciers, valleys, meadows and dense forests of birch, deodar and pines the holy Bhagirathi flowed down from the high Himalayas. It rushed down from high ridges raging, roaring and splashing white foam and water on rocks trees and shrubs. In meadows and gentle valleys it slowed down and meandered. Her celestial beauty and serenity attracted many sages, hermits and ascetics who settled near her bank for meditation and god realization.

Several other rivers, its tributaries, meet her on her long journey to the sea. The first to meet is Kedar Ganga at Gangotri, and then Jahnvi at Bhairon Ghati, Pilangana at Malla two miles from Bhatwari,. Asiganga at Uttarkasi and Bhilangna at Tehri, a town now submerged under the newly constructed Tehri Dam. At Deoprayag Bhagirathi meets her sister Alaknanda which comes from the Satopanth glacier. The combined river is then called Ganga till she meets the sea.

On reaching the plains Ganga happened to flood the place where king Jahnu was performing a yagya. "Ganga", Jahnu thought, "is full of ego and proud of her strength". In a rage of anger he swallowed the river. The sages who were following the holy river with reverence prayed to the king to release the river for the good of the earth and said that she will hence forth be called his daughter. The king agreed and took out Ganga from his ear. Ganga now added one more name and is also called Jahnvi.

Bhagirath took the Holy Ganga straight near the sea where the ashes of his ancestors were lying in a big heap. Ganga flooded the place, washed away the remains of the departed princes and liberated them. Bhagirath offered holy water to his ancestors and prayed for the peace of their souls. Brahma, whose blessings were with Bhagirath through out his great mission, appeared before him. He praised him for his penance and said. " Bhagirath!, Ganga will now bear your name and will be called Bhagirathi". Ganga is called by many divine names like Vishnupada,Tripathga, Jahnvi and Bhagirathi.

And so the legend of Ganga passes on from generation to generation and has become a living element, a part of our life. Even the skeptics wonder," what is it that has captivated the hearts of millions from immemorial past, and what has drawn them to her holy banks since antiquity?:. The legend glorifies the purity, divinity and sublimity of the holy mother, it speaks of the heroic efforts of king Bhagirath, who left his kingdom and comforts and with undaunted determination turned impossibility into a reality. He brought the divine goddess from heaven to earth for the prosperity and liberation of mankind. Sages have composed hymns which the devotees sing in their morning prayers.

"There is no shrine holier than Ganga,
No god greater than Keshava,
And no hymn more sacred than Gayatri.

With Geeta, Ganga, Govind,
And Gayatri in your heart,
It is liberation,
No rebirth again

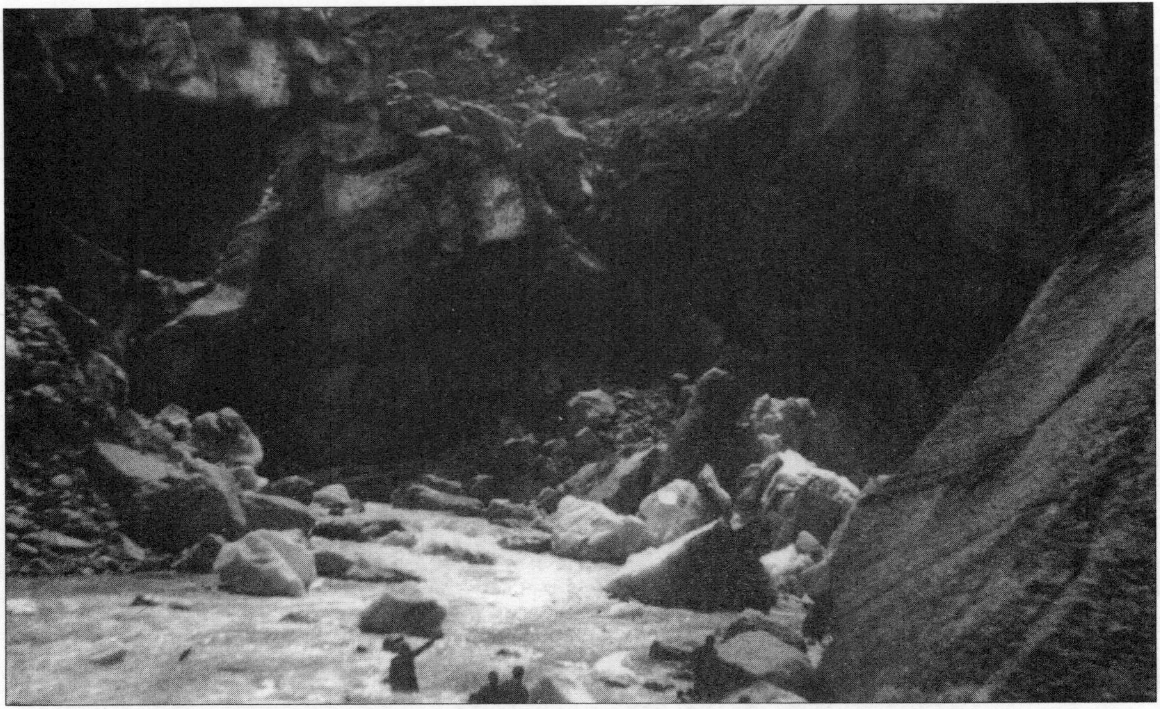

GAUMUKH

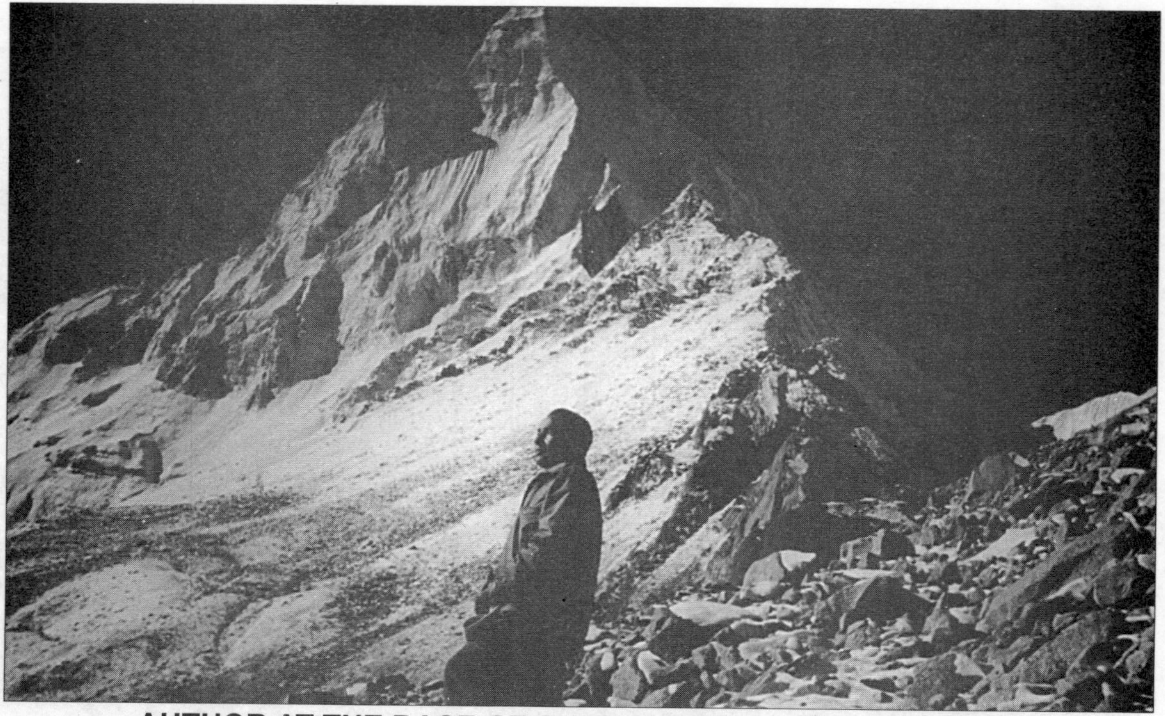

AUTHOR AT THE BASE OF SHIVLING PEAK, TAPOVAN, 1962

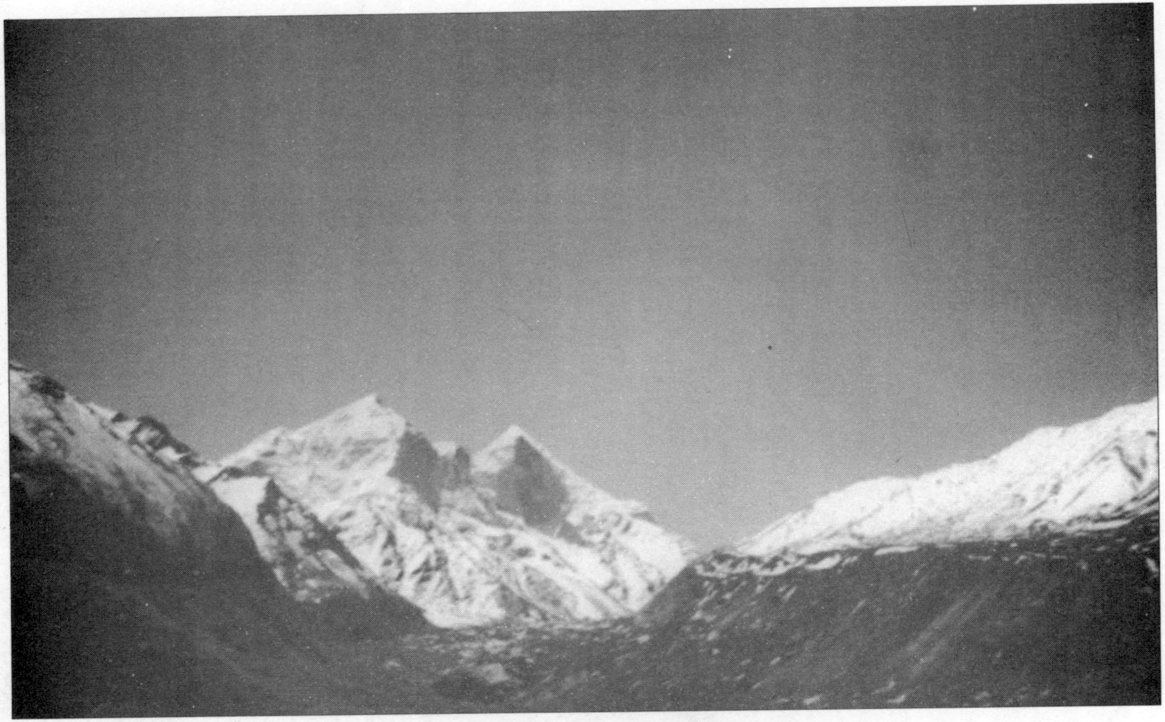

BHAGRITH PEAKS

26

Tracing the Source: Gangotri, Gaumukh and Tapovan

A delightful journey through the serene, celestial valley brings the pilgrim to the holy shrine of Gangotri which is situated at an altitude of 3140 meters above sea level, amid sylvan surroundings. It was thousands of years ago, that Bhagirath, the King Emperor of Bharat, entered this quiet mountainous valley of glittering snow peaks, passed through the dense forests and chose this tranquil, holy; spot for his penance. The Goddess Ganga, pleased with Bhagirath's austerities and prayers, ascended here from heaven and followed Bhagirath to Ganga Sagar to liberate his 60,000 ancestors and give life and prosperity to the parched land of north India. The glacier, the source of Ganga, has now receded 18km back to Gaumukh.

The rock on which Bhagirath sat for his long penance is called Bhagirath Shilla and is close to the temple.

I visited Gangotri in July1959 for the first time. It was then a 123km, journey on foot, from Dharasu and attracted lesser number of pilgrims than Badrinath. I met Hareshwar Prasad Semwal an old priest of Gangotri who was our family priest. He told me that the present temple was constructed by the king of Jaipur in the early Twentieth Century, after the old temple built by Amar Singh Thapa, a Gurkha commander, during the Gurkha occupation of Garhwal, in the early Nineteenth Century, was damaged by heavy snow fall. The Semwal Brahmins of Mukhwa village are the priests of the temple.

The temple opens on the auspicious day of *Akshaya Tritiya* which normally falls in the last week of April or first week of May and is closed for winter after Deepawali in November. Ganga is worshipped in her Mukhwa temple during winter.

Gangotri is surrounded by the snow covered Rocky Mountains. The temple and the small town is on the right bank of the Bhagirathi which comes speedily from Gaumukh and cascades down to Gauri Kund in small attracting falls just below the temple. It is a green tranquil valley, covered with deodar forests which are now dwindling down due to increased construction of houses and demand for fuel.

A beautiful marble idol of goddess Ganga, adorned with gorgeous clothes and jewels is placed on a pedestal, inside the temple. The other idols placed there are of goddess Yamuna, Maha Laxmi, Sraswati, king Bhagirath and Adi Guru Shankaracharya.

After bathing in the icy water of the sacred river, the devotees go to the temple, with their offerings, in a queue to worship the goddess. The priests perform pooja (worship) of the Mother both in the morning and evening. The most attractive ritual, performed each evening, is *Arati,*"an ending part of the worship, by moving several lighted wicks circularly round the idol of the goddess".

The priests and the devotees sing songs of the glory of the mother.

The holy water of Bhagirathi Ganga is believed to contain medicinal properties. It does not contaminate for several months. The pilgrims carry sealed bottles of Ganga water as a holy present to their friends and relations.

Gauri Kund

Named after Gauri, the consort of Lord Shiva, Gauri Kund is a thrilling spot some 300 meters down the temple. Tearing hard rocks and cascading down, the turbulent Ganga passes through a narrow gorge. The whole river drops straight, forty feet below, into a deep round pool of hard granite rock, with roaring sound, spraying thick foam around. A close look at the bottom, where the stream splashes, gives a glimpse of a raised round rock, resembling Shiv lingam.

There is a belief among the devotees that Ganga offers herself to Shiva here hence the water below this point is not offered to the Shiva temple at Rameshwaram, far in the south, near the sea coast. The devotees take water from up stream.

Patangana

Patangana is a picturesque place at a distance of one km from Gauri Kund. Surrounded by a thick forest of Deodar trees, it is a natural pavement of flat wide rocks, stretching to a long distance, along the left bank of the river. An ideal place for meditation, I wish this quiet setting in nature be spared from greedy human eye and not used for any settlement. Let it remain a place of solitude and bliss, a breathing space for the congested Gangotri Town.

Gaumukh

Devi Sureshwari Bhagwati Gangey, Tribhuwan tarini taral tarangey,

Shankar mauli viharini vimaley, mam matirastaina taw pad kamaley.

(Shankarecharaya)

Oh divine goddess of the gods, Gangey! Liberator of the three worlds,
You are pure and beautiful and with your bright splendid waves,
You delightfully roam about the matted hair of Shiva.
May my mind stay with reverence at thy lotus feet?

In one of his finest prayers, Adi Guru Shankaracharya has eulogized the celestial beauty, divine glory and purifying attributes of the holy Ganga.

I had heard about the grandeur and majestic beauty of Gaumukh, the source of Ganga which is 18km from Gangotri and was eagerly looking for the day I would touch the holy feet of the mother at her source.

It was mid September 1962, nice time to visit the Harsil valley, Gangotri and Gaumukh. After visiting the villages Sukhi, Jhala, Mukhwa and Dharali I reached Gangotri in the third week of the month and met Swami Sundaranand with whom I was quite close. An ardent disciple of the great sage Tapoban Maharaj, Swami Sundaranand lives in his quiet hermitage, on the left bank of the Bhagirathi. He has travelled widely in the high Himalayan region, scaled the Nanda Devi peak and has undertaken the hazardous mountainous journey from Gangotri to Badrinath through the 19,000ft high Kalandi

Pass, many times. A skilled photographer, he has captured the exquisite beauty of the majestic Himalayan peaks, glaciers and other beauty spots in his rare slides which he often displays on his projector to interested lovers of the Himalayas.

I was lucky to have Swamiji's wonderful company on my first pilgrimage to Gaumukh and Tapoban. It was a partially cloudy morning when we left for Gaumukh at nine in the morning. There was no regular beaten path. We had to find our way along the slender Bhagirathi, walk carefully on rubble and at times take a precarious climb over steep rocks and huge boulders that had slipped from the high mountains. After an arduous march of nine km, we reached Chirvasa at four in the afternoon. Surrounded by thick pine trees (called chir by local people) Chirvasa (abode of chir trees) is a beautiful camping place. There was an old dharamshala but we chose to pitch our small alpine tents on the open ground. Some shepherds who had just descended from the high alpine grasslands with their flocks were camping there. They offered us goat milk which was very delicious.

Next morning we marched to Bhojvasa. The birch forest now replaces the pines which extend up to Bhojvasa. Because of the abundance of the bhoj trees (birch) in those days, this place was named Bhojvasa. The thin layers of the bark of bhoj tree are called Bhoj Patras and were used for writing in the good old days when paper was scarce. There was a log bridge on the Bhagirathi few meters below Bhojvasa. We crossed over to the right bank, reached Pushavasa and camped there. Full of green grass and small flowers, it is a beautiful place from where you can see a part of the gigantic Gangotri glacier, Bhagirath peaks and Shivling peak.

We had a plan to go to Tapoban the next morning, stay there for a day and visit Gaumukh on our return but I could not resist the temptation of Goumukh, so close now. We took a hurried lunch and an hour's pleasant walk took us to Gaumukh.

Gaumukh open up suddenly when you are close to it. It is a sight unimaginable and indescribable, a great wonder of nature. The gigantic glacier glistens with century old blocks of white and blue ice, forming a wall, more than a hundred meters high and the holy Ganga rushes out of a big cave 30ft wide, just below. Several blocks of ice that fall from the glacier continue floating on the surface of the river till they are carried away by the flow. A mixed feeling of awe, reverence and wonder made me speechless and I continued gazing with ecstasy and amazement at the holy mother emerging on earth from the mouth of the sacred cow.

Aurobindo, in his book," The Secret of the Veda" interprets the inner sense of the word Gau as the ray of the sun at dawn, a divine illumination. Gaumukh thus signifies the first touch of light the holy river gets after coming out of the dark recesses of the giant Gangotri glacier extending for miles where the Ganga is shrouded in darkness. Here at Gaumukh she comes out from the illumined mouth, the mouth of the dawn.

In this visit I did notice the snout in a round shape, similar to that of the mouth of cow but in my subsequent visits in 1988 and 1994 the shape was quite different. The orifice continues changing its shape.

Whatever meaning you ascribe to the word, Gaumukh, the holy source of the Bhagirathi, is unique in its grandeur, majesty and sanctity. A holy dip at this odd hour of the evening though most desired was not suitable. I postponed it for my return visit from Tapoban. Bowing to the serene, divine goddess we returned to our tents at Pushpavasa.

The morning was cloudy. We left for Tapovan after breakfast. It was a gradual ascent and climbing at this height of over 12,000ft above sea level was difficult. Our speed slowed down. Thick clouds started gathering and we were engulfed by a dense fog. Visibility was reduced to four or five meters. There was no regular path and we were groping in the dark fog. Swamiji who had visited Tapovan many times was acquainted with the terrain. After a tiresome journey, we reached Tapovan at three in the afternoon. We, however, had no idea of the topography of the place due to dense fog. Swamiji showed a cave where we took our lunch and rested.

The porters who were very slow reached at five in the evening. We pitched our small tents and went inside. It was drizzling and cold.

We were now at a height of 14,000ft above sea level. I had a disturbed sleep. I woke up at two in the night and saw some light. I came out of the tent. The moon had just come out of the clouds. I was wonderstruck by the scene around. I found myself in the midst of a galaxy of glistening snow peaks. At a distance of about two hundred meters, there stood a huge mountain, with its shining snow peak, soaring high into the sky. On my left was a massive glacier, stretching like a gigantic crocodile along the Tapovan plane. Behind the glacier three beautiful peaks were bathed in moonlight and scattering their sweet smile all around. Was it a dream or reality? I could not believe my eyes. I was in a wonderland and as I was witnessing the panoramic view that stretched in front of me, thick clouds covered the moon and it became dark. Alone in a fairyland, a sudden fear crept into my heart. Shivering with cold, I slipped into my bed with my mind full of the scenic beauty that lulled me to sleep.

It rained in the night and there was fresh snow on the higher ridges. I narrated my experience of the night to Swamiji. He told me that the peak rising from the Tapovan plane on the right is the Shivling peak and on the left the Gangotri glacier. The three peaks behind the glacier are the Bhagirath peaks. We were busy in our talks when the porters who were ill-equipped for the sudden inclement weather stood before us.

"We spent a cold sleepless night". One of them said. He requested us to pack our luggage so that we may leave for Gangotri before an imminent snow fall which would make our movement very difficult.

The night's scene had captivated my mind and I did not like to leave the place without seeing its splendid grandeur and beauty in full.

"I am confident, the weather will clear up by tomorrow", I told them. I requested them to stay and promised to give double wages for the day. They agreed and the problem was solved.

There was intermittent rain the whole day followed by a snow fall in the evening which continued till twelve in the night. Before going to sleep, I prayed for a sunny morrow. I woke up at five in the morning and was overjoyed to see a clear blue sky. It was after 38 hours that I could get a full view of my picturesque surroundings. The whole place was white with fresh snow.

Tapovan

At an altitude of 14,000ft above sea level, Tapovan is an exquisitely beautiful spot between the Gangotri glacier and the Shiv Ling peak. As its name reveals, Tapovan is a sacred land, land of gods, a quiet place for meditation and penance. Surrounded by dazzling snow peaks, it is the base of the lofty Shiv Ling peak 6540m high. The Gangotri glacier forms its north western boundary. Behind the glacier are three majestic snow peaks, Bhagirath (I)6510 M, Bhagirath (II), 6450 m, Bhagirath (III) 6860 m high, standing like celestial sentinels, scattering their silver radiance in the blue sky.

Opposite Tapovan on the North is another extensive plain, Nandanvan, with Chaturangi glacier on its west. The high mountainous route to Badrinath passes along the bank of this glacier.

The Gangotri Glacier

The Gangotri glacier is one of the longest glaciers of the Himalayan range and extends from the western slop of Chaukhamba peaks to Gaumukh. It is about 30 km long and 2 km wide. Several other glaciers, namely Raktverna, Chaturangi, Nilamber and Pitamber are its tributary glaciers and feed it. Gaumukh, the 100 m high grey blue wall of ice is the snout of the glacier. I strolled over the glacier to some distance. It is a solid mass of hard ice mixed with mud, rubble and rocks. The ages old ice looks black and at places blue. The GangotrI glacier is the perpetual reservoir of holy water, drained by Bhagirathi and is a blessing for north India.

We spent the whole forenoon searching for vantage places to take photographs, climbed over a high ridge adjoining the Shiv Ling peak, from where I took nice photographs of various peaks. The massive Shiv Ling peak was just in front of me.

I found myself completely lost in the divine wonder of the Himalayas. The dream of my younger days was fulfilled. I sat watching the splendid panorama from the high ridge. My eyes rested on the Gangotri glacier. The legend of Ganga's descent on earth came to my mind. The massive glacier looked like the matted locks of Lord Shiva where Ganga lost her way. Baghirath's earnest prayers melted Shiva's heart and he gave her a passage.

With a reluctant heart I left Tapovan in the evening. We camped at Gaumukh. It was again a clear morning. Gaumukh is extremely cold due to its being surrounded by high mountains and the icy cave. The first rays of the sun come after nine in the morning. We waited for the warmth of the sun to enable us take a holy dip. It was thrilling to see the blocks of white ice floating on the surface of the speeding river which is almost waist deep here. I had to gather some courage to take the first dip after which the body was acclimatized, and it was easy and pleasant to take two more dips. The body felt rejuvenated after the dips. The porters were now very happy and they too enjoyed the holy dips. I lit a candle and worshipped the mother goddess.

We left the holy source in the evening, halted at Chirvasa and reached Gangotri the next day for our onward journey to Bhatwari.

The charm of the Harsil valley, Gangotri and Gaumukh remained in my mind long after I left uttarkashi district in 1964. A chance meeting with Swami Sunderanand, in a city bus at Delhi in December 1987, revived the old memories. He invited me to Gangotri next summer.

I visited Gangotri and Gaumukh in June 1988 and then again in May 1994. I found an enormous change. Change is the law of nature and there are reasons for the change. Communication is one of the important factors that brings rapid change in the over all system and structure of a region and its social and cultural life.

Gangotri was connected by motor road in June 1985, after the completion of a 100 meters long and 5;5 meters wide bridge over the turbulent Jahnwai river at Bharon Ghati. The thin old iron ropes hanging on tall deodar poles, remnant of the Wilson age had disappeared. The new motor road bridge is said to be the highest bridge of the world, with the river flowing 103 feet below.

Travel to the holy shrine of Gangotri has become easy. Gangotri is flooded with an unmanageable rush of the pilgrims and tourists during pilgrim season. Several haphazard constructions have come up to cater for their needs and spin money. The town has become too congested and all the dirty discharge of the crowded place is flowing into the river. Hundreds of vehicles bring thousands of pilgrims each day. This has ruined the majestic charm of the Himalayan shrine and polluted the air and holy water of the Ganga. Effective regulations are needed to save the fragile ecology of the holy place.

Gaumukh

There was a time when a visit to Gaumukh was an adventure full of hardships and undertaken only by a few hardy devotees who went with boundless faith in the divinity of the holy mother. They had to carry with them their essential requirements of food, clothes and bedding. A six feet wide path with restaurants and facilities for a night's stay at Chirvasa and Bhojvasa has made the trip easy. There is a stream of people, young and old, going to Gaumukh each day from May to October. The restaurants are consuming quintals of fire wood and the rich forests have depleted. Bhojvasa was once proud of its dense birch forests. You can now count just a few trees here and there standing naked with their thin beautiful paper like layers stripped from their stems by crazy passers by. It takes a long time for the plants to grow and reach their normal height in the high altitudes and if this depletion goes on unchecked and proper steps are not taken to plant and preserve these valuable forests this green valley will meet the fate of Badrinath valley where there is no vegetation now. The Gangotri glacier has receded far behind during the past decades and the influx of a greater number of people, cutting down of trees and burning of fire wood has accelerated the speed. If this mad rush goes on the perennial reservoir of water will dry and Bhagirathi, the river of gods, will disappear from this earth and no Bhagirath can bring her back. There should be a strict check on the flow and conduct of visitors. No construction activity should be allowed beyond Gangotri and a strict watch be kept on the felling of trees.

The Gangotri National Park

The government has declared the whole area from Gangotri to Nandanvan a national park to check the deterioration of the eco system of the sacred region. The place has suffered vast degradation and depletion of forests during the last decades. An effective management of the project will ensure rejuvenation, conservation and preservation of the fragile eco system of this Himalayan region and save the glacier and the holy Ganga. Our scriptures and seers have attributed the image of the supreme goddess to Ganga. She is the incarnation of mother Sati, the consort of Shiva. Let us maintain her purity and holiness. Let us go to her holy abode like sages of ancient times and preserve nature's harmony and peace.

27

Art and Culture of Uttaranchal Hills

Having sung the glory of the Himalayas, its people and the Ganga, I come to the origin and formation of this superb creation of God, its art, culture and folk lore.

Handiwork of the master artist, the anatomy of the Himalayas is a work which of all others expresses a nakedness of the region's total grandeur. Going back to the beginning we find that a hundred million years ago in the cretaceous age when sea had spread over the land, the entire Himalayan region was covered by the Thethy's sea. At that time the subcontinent of India formed a part of that super landmass known as Gondwana Land.

During the late Cretaceous period, the Indian landmass travelled in a series of tectonic movements till it made contact with the Eurasian continent. Ensuing uplift and horizontal thrust movements that resulted from this collusion raised the floor of the sea to crumple and fold and thus form the Himalayas.

In the course of its formative period the entire topography must have presented a raw, bleak and barren picture. It awaited the handiwork of nature to impart to the scene the total final touches of its present day makeup.

As the Himalayas rose, the whole of river system developed. The sea started receding and most of the territory bore a green mantle of plants and trees followed by aquatic life, birds and animals. Life evolved further and man stepped into the arena and dominated the existing panorama. Men found safe abode in the rich fertile valleys and gentle hill slops. With their simple hand tools, ingenuity, labour and skill they converted bare mountains into fine terraced fields, grew different grains, fruits, vegetables and reared cattle and sheep. The rich forests provided items essential for subsistence. Permanent settlements became the centre of their socio economic culture.

The peace and tranquility of Himalayas, its glittering snow peaks, springs and rivers and exuberant vegetation attracted the sages, saints and hermits who spent their long lives in the pursuit of art, literature, philosophy and spiritual knowledge. It was here that the four Vedas were revealed to the sages and the Mahabharat and Puranas were written. Profoundly steeped in their religious convictions they established the four Dhams at Jamnotri, Gangotri, Kedarnath and Badrinath,. where flock thousands of devotees each year. There are several temples where the deep sighing of every gust of wind conveys the eco of Shiva, goddess Parvati, Durga,and Lord Vishnu.

The events related in Puranas, Ramayan, Mahabharat which were written thousands of years ago and those in Kalidas's epics in the later age that have surfaced in previous chapters show the popularity of the region throughout India during long past. It was here that king Bhagirath performed penance and Ganga descended from heaven, Hanuman took the Sanjeewani herb and Pandavas wandered in search of Shiva and traced him at Kedarnath. All these and Ashok's Edicts at Kalsi in Dehradun district of a much later age prove that rich culture and civilization prospered in Garhwal and Kumaon area much before the Christ era. It excelled in art, literature, drama, philosophy and spiritual learning.

Coming to much later age we find that several kings right from the time of Katyuries who ruled the region from 850 A. D. to 1050 A. D and other rulers who followed gave patronage to artists, poets and architects.

Maula Ram has been one of the finest artists during the last half of the eighteenth century. He lived in the court of the Garhwal kings at Srinagar (Garhwal). Art and culture reached its zenith during his time. He was followed by many of his followers. Mukandi Lal Barister did commendable work in the collection of his rare paintings. These paintings were published in his historical book "Garhwal Paintings" in 1968. He was the man who brought the famous works of Maula Ram on the world map. Maula Ram was a poet and historian as well.

Sculptures

Uttaranchal is full of temples with magnificent idols carved out of fine smooth stones. The idols of Nar Singh Bhawan at Joshimath and that of Lord Vishnu at Rudranath are the finest idols I have seen. Some of the old temples known for their rich architect are at Kedarnath, Badrinath, Jageshwer, Bageshwar, Champawat, Gopeshwar, Joshimath, Lakhamandal and Pandukeshwer. The architecture of these temples radiates the holiness and glory of their superb Himalayan surroundings.

Folk Songs and Folk Dances

The natural beauty of the Himalayas reflects in the folk songs and dances of the hill people. Songs come out like natural springs from the hearts of simple village folk. The traditional songs, dances and instrumental music make life sweet and give support to people during their sorrows and sufferings. They bring harmony in life and keep people in a loving bond. They are an essential part of the community life.

Songs are based on nature, the birds who build their nests in the village surroundings and sing their sweet songs, trees and flowers. Some songs are based on seasons like spring, winter, rains, some depict the hard life led by men and women, and some remind married women of their parents in the distant land. There are songs sung during worship of a deity, songs sung at the marriage ceremony, songs narrating valor of brave people like Madho Singh Bhandari, Teelu Rauteli a brave girl who fought the Katyuri king and died a valiant death.

There are several forms of folk dances. The most common dance is the Pandav dance which is performed all over the hills during melas and festivals. It is accompanied by the beating of drums in a rhythmic tone. The drummers sing the songs of the valor of the Pandavas.

The Himalaya has been symbolized as father of Uma and father in law of Lord Shiva. Most of the folk songs are sung in praise of Shiva and his consort Uma (Parvati).

An attempt was made to revive the rich heritage in the border blocks by Dr Sampoornand, the chief minister of U. P. during late fifties and good work was done. After the creation of Uttaranchal state folk songs and dances are now being revived. They are frequently performed during functions in towns and villages. Let us preserve our rich heritage in its pure classical form.

For want of major industries the hill region especially the remote areas still suffer from poverty and unemployment. Tourism is catching on and like a golden magnet is attracting visitors from all over the world. Mountaineering, trekking and white water rafting is drawing those who are interested and will in near future be yet another source of employment for the locals.

Be that as it may, the fact remains that the eye of any visitor to these parts in the Himalayas is always held in thrall by the rustic charm of its people, their customs and their apparel. The alluring charm remains in the gaiety, honesty and cheerfulness of the people. It is fervently hoped that in the midst of our changing times and materialistic modern values these good people will remain what they have always been, kindly, likable lot.

28

The Hill Women

The beauty of the Himalayan hills finds its reflection and expression in the charm and beauty of its women who mostly are fair coloured with well proportioned features.

Agriculture is the main occupation in hills. Industries have just touched the fringes of Deheradun, Haridwar. UdhamSingh Nagar districts and some towns of Tarai and Bhabar.

The hill women are the backbone of this agriculture economy. They play an important role through their active participation in major agriculture activities. They are busy from the break of the day till late at night. Their day begins with grinding flour, fetching water from the village spring, husking rice, milking cows, collecting fuel and fodder, cooking meals, tending cattle and rearing children. They attend to various agriculture operations like sowing, weeding, hoeing, paddy transplantation, harvesting, threshing and winnowing. Males just do the ploughing and some other work like mending the irrigation channels or keeping a watch over the harvest. Most of the males migrate to the plains to earn money to support the family as the produce is not sufficient for the year. It is as such a money order economy. The young hill men are mostly employed in the army, police and in other jobs. This migration of males adds to the workload and responsibility of the women.

Despite their major contribution to the family they have a small share in social status. Their economic and social role has not been recognized. With the expansion of education the trend is changing. Among the school going children now the number of girls exceeds that of boys and some of them are finding employment as teachers in village primary schools.

I end the chapter with a poem written by me long back in praise of the hill women.

God's Image

Oh look the sky is thick with clouds.
The rains have set and fields are ploughed.
Full of water the fields are muddy,
The maidens are busy planting paddy.
They sing and plant the seedlings green,
Their melodies ring in hills serene.
While husking rice or grinding flour,
Collecting fuel or gathering grass.
In distant woods or pastures green,
You know what songs the maidens sing.
They sing in chorus with natural ease,
Their songs delight like morning breeze.
What songs they sing in distant land,
To me a riddle to understand.
An echo perhaps of their daily life,
Of rugged struggle too full of strife.
Their songs may tell some lover's tale,
Resounding melodies in hills and dales.
Unfulfilled dreams of life may cast,

Or memories sweet of life long past.
Their songs unveil their natural charm,
Attuned in harmony with dexterous arms.
From bosom warm a spontaneous flow,
Like sparkling springs from earth below.
In struggle of life hardy they grow,
They earn their bread by sweat of brow.
Their simple ways without a show,
Their hearts as pure as Himalayan snow.
Their honest faces shinning as stars,
In human form god's image they are.

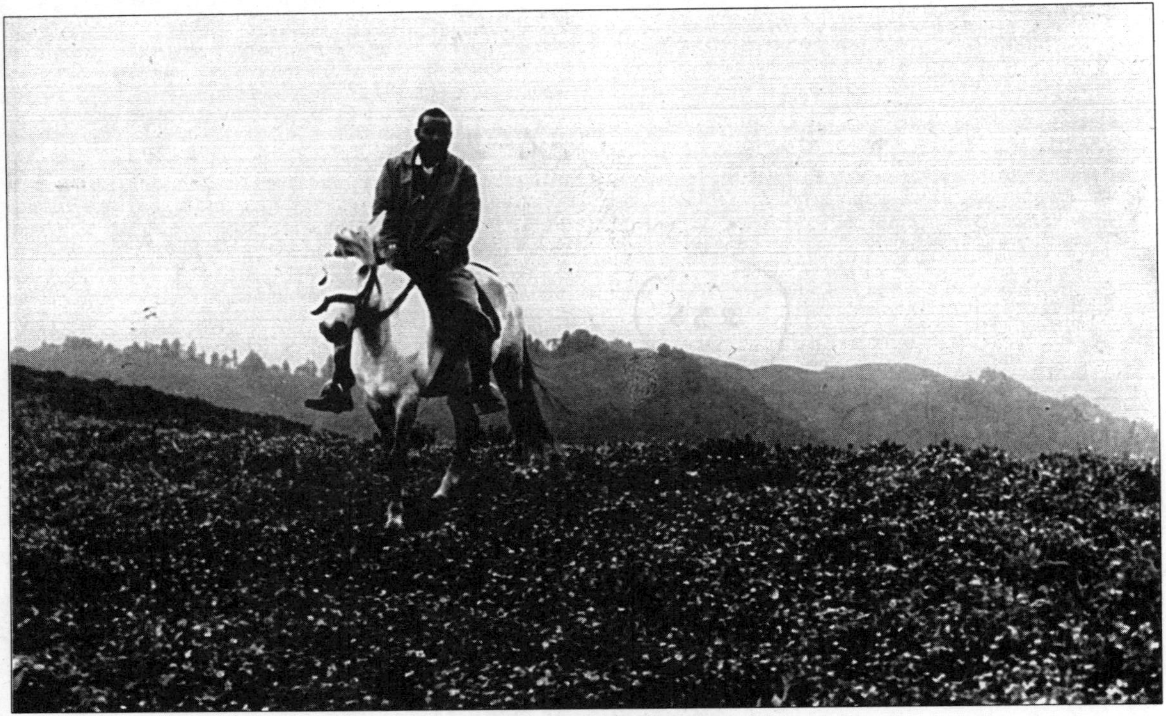

NEELU MY HORSE

29

Days with Neelu My Horse

The government provided two horses to us to facilitate touring in Bhatwari, the border block of Uttarkashi district. It was not connected by motor roads in the year 1958. One of them named Neelu remained my companion for six years that I was there. The animal does not know its legal owner. For it, he who feeds, loves, cares and looks after it is its owner. Since I did all this, it took me as its master and I had a right to call it my horse.

Neelu was bluish, young and agile. Bhurey, the other one was gray, aged and plump. I saw them grazing in a field nearby a day after I joined after my transfer from Joshimath. Neelu caught my eye. On a close look I found it's back badly scratched. Blood was oozing out and flies hovering over it. The sight moved me. I called the syce.

"Do you see something wrong with this horse?"

"Yes sir it has scratches its back".

"Who is responsible and why have you not taken it to the hospital?"

My words shook him. Putting his hands on his forehead he spoke softly.

"What can I do sir, it is a good horse to ride and every one prefers it. The other is dull and seldom used."

"So this is the reward you are giving to the poor animal. This is merciless. You will kill it. Take it to the veterinary hospital at once and get its wounds cleaned and dressed."

I followed him, met the veterinary surgeon and requested him for his personal attention.

The horse was given a rest. I supervised its treatment and feeding.

It took a month for the wounds to heal and hair to grow. The vet certified it fit for riding but I was apprehensive and cautious.

I bought some soft cotton pads and instructed the syce to put them below the saddle to avoid friction.

Neelu was now quite healthy and friendly with me. I ensured that the syce scrubbed and gave a massage to both the horses regularly.

One evening I took Neelu for riding. Long rest had made it restive and unmanageable. I had done lot of riding in my younger days but it was long past. I felt my body aching but after some days I gained rhythm with its trot, canter and gallop and became a perfect rider.

As days passed we were perfectly in tune. I knew its gestures and body language and it understood my words and cautions. If some villages were unapproachable for the horse or there were standing crops along the way I would leave Neelu on the way side and ask it to be there till I returned. It would be there!

Uttarkashi, the district headquarter is 18 miles from Bhatwari. I had to go there quite often to visit villages scattered on both sides of the road and attend staff meetings. On my way I used to stop at Biya, some eight miles from Bhatwari where Himmat Singh a jolly good old man had a teashop. Here I gave Neelu some gram and jaggery. My next stop would be at Abbal Singh's shop at Kheri. The horse would get some grass there while I talked to the villagers. The horse would feel fresh and contented.

One day Dabral, subdivisional magistrate of Bhatwari took Neelu to Uttarkashi. When he reached Biya the horse stopped and would not move. Himmat Singh recognized the horse.

"The horse will not move unless it gets gram and jaggary." He requested Dabral to get down and have a cup of tea while the horse took its meal. So it did at Kheri. Dabral told me that I had spoiled the habit of the horse. I told him that the horse needs proper feed and rest to keep it fit for riding.

One day I was going to Jamak, a village across the Bhagirathi River, 10 miles from my headquarters. An old suspension bridge over the river was unsafe for animals. It was a cold January morning. The syce was with the other horse. I stopped at a shop near Maneri. I wanted to leave the horse with the shopkeeper and take it back on my return from Jamak. I requested the shopkeeper to look after it till my return. Harikrishna, sarpanch of a nearby village was sitting there with some villagers.

"Why are you not taking the horse to Jamak sir? I took my buffalo on that bridge the day before". He requested me to have a cup of tea.

'I do not want to take the risk; I'd better leave it here".

"When the buffalo can cross it why not your horse sir?" he smiled and spoke with conviction.

I had my doubts but I do not know why his words changed my mind. I left with the horse.

When I approached the bridge I got down and took the reins in my hand. As I stepped on to the bridge the horse shook its head and was reluctant to move. It sensed some trouble. Harikrishna's words were in my mind and I overruled Neelu's gestures. I pulled the reins and the horse followed. I had hardly gone a few steps that I found the planks at the center tilting. I thought of turning back but the bridge was narrow and it was not possible for the horse to take a turn. The horse would lose its balance and slip. Turning back was more dangerous than going ahead. I was in a dilemma. There was no choice and I continued my steps. Suddenly there was a sound of the slip of a hoof. The bridge shook. I shuddered; we are going down in the river in a second, I thought. I held my breath and tried to gather courage. I had no guts to look back. I tightened the reins. I do not know how the horse regained balance. I continued walking. By God's grace we were at the other end. I stood motionless near a pillar with the horse by my side. I was tense and saw the horse shivering. Its whole body was sweating profusely. Neelu was panting and its legs were trembling as if it had come from a race. Its wet eyes looked at me with a strange expression accusing me of my folly. I patted Neelu, put my arms round its neck, wiped its sweat, and thanked Neelu for saving both of us. It was God's mercy and a narrow escape.

After some rest we climbed and reached the village on the ridge. Fateh Singh, the Pradhan, who was waiting for me was surprised to see the horse with me.

"How could you bring the horse on that bridge? It was unsafe".

"Yes, it was my silly mistake. I believed Harikrishan who met me at Maneri and told me that he had taken his buffalo on the bridge the day before and the horse could easily cross the bridge".

"A day before?" exclaimed Fateh Singh. "It was some three months back and the bridge was then in a better condition. In village parlance day before means some months back".

"That was my blunder".

I attended to my work and left the horse with Fateh Singh.

"I will send someone to look after it. He will bring it back after the bridge is repaired and fit for the horse to cross"

You need not worry sir; it will take long time for the bridge to be repaired. I will bring the horse by a different route that I know and avoid the bridge.

I returned back in the evening. Fateh Singh brought the horse the third day.

After touring for a week I was returning to my headquarters. Neelu was galloping fast on a level road. Suddenly a man appeared from a bend on the other side, dragging a big bundle of reeds. The queer sound and dust alarmed the horse. It startled, shied and raised its front legs with a jerk. I lost my grip but some how managed to stick to the saddle and saved myself from a fall. I asked the man not to drag the bundle till I was out of sight. As the horse started galloping the man dragged the bundle. This time the horse totally lost its balance and threw me down. My back was hurt. I stood up in pain and anger and whipped the horse. Neelu looked at me with apologetic eyes as if admitting its fault. I felt sorry for losing my temper, patted Neelu and promised not to whip it again.

"I had told you not to drag the bundle till I was out of sight", I shouted at the man. "You alarmed the horse and I got hurt".

The man apologized, stood at a corner and requested me to ride.

It is more than 45 years now. When I get pain in my back I am reminded of the incident and fond memory of Neelu stirs my heart.

It was autumn. Both the horses were grazing on the slope of a ridge. The grass had started turning gray. Bhurey, the other horse came near a slippery rock, lost its balance and slipped down it. It broke its back badly and died. I was at Uttarkashi that day and was informed on phone. I instructed my staff to get its postmortem done by the veterinary surgeon and bury the horse at a proper place.

It was a sad day for us but very tragic for Neelu who lost its mate and was witness to the whole scene. I returned back the next day. The syce told me that Neelu had not touched a single blade of grass and the soaked gram. It stood still on the spot the whole day. The next day too it went to the same spot and stood motionless.

A change was necessary. I had to inspect some projects near Maneri and I took Neelu with me. I stayed there for two days. The horse now started taking grass and gram.

At night the syce tied the horse outside the outhouse where he was staying. In the morning he found the horse missing. It broke its rope and ran away. The syce got worried and made a thorough search up to Uttarkashi. He informed me at about seven in the morning.

"The horse has run away. I have gone up to Uttarkashi to search it sir, but found no trace".

"You went in the wrong direction. Go to the spot where its mate died you will find it there". The syce brought the horse from there in the evening.

It took several days for the horse to become normal. I was moved to see the deep love among animals.

Firm, sure footed and balanced, Neelu was sober, faithful and obedient. It was its sheer firmness that saved us on that fateful day on Zamak Bridge. It could negotiate difficult tracks with perfect ease and follow me wherever I went. Neelu remained my sweet companion for six long years at Bhatwari. I still remember Neelu's big eyes, loving looks and cherish its memory.

Epilogue

It has been my pride and pleasure to have served the distinguished people of Garhwal to whom I give my grateful thanks. My thanks are also due to the kind readers who have spent idle hours going through this narrative. I express my heartfelt gratitude to them.

(M P Kuksal)

Index

D

E

F

L

M

S

T

W

Y

Z